Rare Earth Materials Introduction

Table of Contents

1. Introduction to Rare Earth Materials 2
   1.1 Definition and chemical characteristics 2
   1.2 Classification of light and heavy rare earth elements 7
   1.3 Misconceptions about scarcity 12
   1.4 Historical development of rare earth mining 16
2. Geological Formation and Global Distribution 23
   2.1 Mineralogical occurrence and typical host rocks 23
   2.2 Major global deposits 28
   2.3 Extraction potential in under-developed regions 34
   2.4 Factors influencing deposit quality 40
3. Mining and Processing Technologies 47
   3.1 Exploration methods and ore evaluation 47
   3.2 Open-pit and underground mining 52
   3.3 Beneficiation processes 58
   3.4 Hydrometallurgical and pyrometallurgical separation 64
   3.5 Radioactive by-products and handling requirements 70
4. Refining, Metallurgy, and Advanced Processing 78
   4.1 Solvent extraction 78
   4.2 Ion exchange and membrane technologies 84
   4.3 Metal production and alloy fabrication 90
   4.4 Recycling pathways 96
   4.5 Technological barriers in high-purity refinement 103

1. Introduction to Rare Earth Materials
1.1 Definition and chemical characteristics

Rare earth materials form a chemically coherent assemblage that includes the lanthanide series from lanthanum to lutetium, together with scandium and yttrium due to their matching ionic radii and trivalent behaviour in solid-state and aqueous systems. Their defining feature lies within the 4f electron shell. The 4f electrons remain shielded by filled 5s and 5p orbitals, which restrict external crystal field influence. This shielding produces highly stable and sharply defined electronic energy levels that shape optical, magnetic, and catalytic behaviour. The effective nuclear charge rises across the series. This compresses the 4f orbitals and gives rise to the steady decrease in ionic radii known as the lanthanide contraction. The contraction influences coordination environments, bond lengths, and partition coefficients in magmatic, metamorphic, and sedimentary systems. The contraction also increases bonding energy in heavier lanthanides and shifts solubility patterns during weathering.

The group displays a dominant trivalent oxidation state under natural and industrial conditions because the energy required to remove a third electron remains lower than the promotion energy required for access to the 5d orbital. Cerium shows stable tetravalent behaviour in oxidative environments, while europium and ytterbium show divalent behaviour under reducing conditions. These exceptions influence geochemical fractionation, as Ce^{4+} becomes immobile during oxidative weathering, while Eu^{2+} partitions into plagioclase through charge balance with Ca^{2+}. The trivalent rare earth ions possess ionic radii that fall within predictable ranges, enabling substitution for Ca^{2+} in apatite, Th^{4+} in monazite, and various medium to large cations in silicates, phosphates, and carbonates. Their placement in host minerals depends on radius ratios, charge balance, and lattice strain energy.

Their electronic structure produces strong paramagnetism in most lanthanides due to unpaired 4f electrons. Gadolinium reaches the maximum magnetic moment because it holds seven unpaired 4f electrons. The same electronic behaviour drives narrow f-f transition lines, which remain only weakly influenced by the surrounding chemical environment. The spectral stability supports rare earth use in phosphors, optical devices, and lasers, where strict control of energy level transitions is required. Their shielding also limits covalent bonding tendencies. It produces predominantly ionic bonds in oxides, phosphates, and carbonates, influencing melting points, vapour pressure behaviour, and phase stability under high temperature.

The group follows predictable trends in hydration energy, formation constants, and complex stability. Trivalent rare earth ions form strong complexes with carbonate, phosphate, and sulphate ligands. These complexes influence transport during surface weathering and dictate the efficiency of industrial leaching methods. Light rare earths form more soluble complexes in mild acidic conditions, while heavy rare earths show increased tendency for adsorption onto clay minerals. These patterns determine the enrichment of heavy elements in ion-adsorption clays of South China and the dispersal of light elements in lateritic profiles. Crystal field splitting plays a limited role in the 4f orbital system, yet minor variations still influence colour, luminescence efficiency, and energy-level lifetimes in solid-state matrices.

Their thermodynamic behaviour underpins metallurgical requirements. Standard reduction potentials remain low, making direct reduction from oxides difficult without strong reductants and controlled atmospheres. Their oxides possess high lattice energies, which raise energy demand during metallothermic or electrolytic reduction. Their halides show improved reducibility, yet still require high-temperature, low-oxygen conditions. Density, vapour pressures, and melting points follow predictable increases across the series, influencing separation, refining, and alloy production processes.

This constellation of traits, driven primarily by the 4f electron system, explains the internal consistency of rare earth chemistry and the fine gradations that separate each element within the group. These properties govern behaviour in geological systems, dictate extraction and refining steps, and define performance in industrial and strategic applications.

Aqueous chemistry controls mobility, solubility, and industrial recoverability of rare earth elements. Trivalent ions undergo strong hydrolysis even at moderate pH values. This drives rapid formation of monomeric and polymeric hydroxo complexes that reduce free ion activity. Hydrolysis constants increase steadily across the series as ionic radii contract and charge density rises. Carbonate, phosphate, sulphate, fluoride, and chloride ligands influence speciation in natural waters and process circuits. Carbonate complexes dominate in many surface environments because atmospheric CO_2 equilibrates with groundwater and produces stable bicarbonate buffering systems. Carbonate ligands stabilise both monodentate and bidentate complexes, which increase mobility of light rare earths. Phosphate interacts strongly with all lanthanides and forms insoluble precipitates that immobilise elements in soils and sediments. Fluoride forms highly stable complexes with heavy rare earths and influences their separation behaviour in fluoride-rich hydrothermal or industrial systems.

Heavy rare earth ions form complexes with higher stability constants due to tighter electrostatic interactions. This drives natural fractionation between light and heavy end members in lateritic, ionic clay, and hydrothermal environments. These variations define the extraction characteristics of Chinese ion-adsorption clays where Y, Dy, Tb, and other heavy rare earths occur in loosely bound states that respond to salt leaching. The weaker lattice binding and stronger surface adsorption of heavy rare earths makes ammonium sulphate and magnesium salts effective in releasing them into solution. Light rare earths remain more tightly bound in resistant minerals such as monazite and bastnäsite and require more aggressive processing.

Magnetic behaviour follows the spin and orbital contributions of 4f electrons and remains largely independent of the surrounding lattice due to shielding. Paramagnetic susceptibility varies predictably across the series. Praseodymium, neodymium, dysprosium, and terbium display strong anisotropic magnetic behaviour when integrated into intermetallic compounds, forming the basis for high-performance permanent magnets. Gadolinium shows a stable half-filled 4f subshell, which drives a peak in magnetic moment and defines its role in magnetic resonance imaging contrast agents. Magnetic ordering temperatures, including Curie and Néel points, vary across lanthanide-based alloys due to interactions between 4f and conduction electrons in metallic matrices.

Optical characteristics arise from f-f transitions that remain Laporte-forbidden and only weakly influenced by external fields. This generates sharp absorption and emission lines with narrow bandwidths. Eu^{3+} produces red emission through the $^5D_0$ to $^7F_2$ transition, while Tb^{3+} generates green emission through the $^5D_4$ to $^7F_5$ pathway. Ce^{3+} exhibits broader emission due to 5d-4f transitions that experience stronger crystal field effects. These optical features underpin phosphor applications in LED lighting, display technologies, and laser components. The shielded f-electron system ensures spectral stability across wide temperature ranges and in various host materials, which strengthens performance in extreme conditions.

Redox behaviour plays a central role in geochemical and industrial systems. Ce^{4+} formation under oxidative conditions removes cerium from solution through precipitation of cerianite. This produces negative Ce anomalies in many geological materials and serves as a redox proxy. Eu^{2+} stabilisation under reducing conditions during plagioclase crystallisation produces positive Eu anomalies. These anomalies trace magmatic evolution pathways and support petrogenetic models. Industrial systems exploit these redox transitions during separation and refining, although strict control of pH, Eh, and ligand composition is required due to narrow stability fields.

Thermodynamic data show systematic progression in hydration energies, Gibbs free energies of formation, and entropy values across the lanthanide series. These parameters influence solubility, stability of complexes, and energy requirements during metallurgical reduction. Knowledge of these trends remains essential for solvent extraction circuit design, ion exchange performance prediction, and high-temperature refining.

Thermodynamic behaviour under industrial conditions determines the feasibility of separation, reduction, and alloy production. Rare earth oxides possess high lattice energies because the trivalent cations form strong ionic bonds with oxygen anions in tightly packed crystal structures. These lattice energies rise across the lanthanide series as ionic radii decrease and electrostatic attraction strengthens. High lattice energies raise the decomposition temperature of the oxides and increase the energy required to convert them into halides or metals. This creates a strong technical barrier during metallothermic and electrolytic reduction, as stable MO, M_2O_3, and mixed oxide phases resist thermal decomposition. Chloride or fluoride routes reduce energy demand, yet still require high-temperature controlled atmospheres due to low vapour pressures and high melting points of the trivalent halides.

Industrial separation circuits rely on predictable changes in complexation strength across the series. Distribution coefficients increase from light to heavy rare earths when using organophosphorus extractants such as tributyl phosphate, phosphinic acids, and phosphonic acids. These extractants form inner-sphere complexes that expose subtle differences in ionic radius and hydration shell structure. The heavy elements transfer more readily into the organic phase due to stronger interactions with the extractant, which allows staged separation in solvent extraction batteries. Ion exchange resins exploit similar trends. Heavy rare earths bind more strongly due to higher charge density, enabling precise stripping sequences with controlled acidity. Membrane-based systems show performance constraints due to low diffusion coefficients of trivalent ions and fouling driven by colloidal hydroxides, but research continues on nanoporous materials with ligand-functionalised channels.

Crystalline and amorphous host phases impose specific coordination geometries that influence behaviour during beneficiation and refining. Light rare earths often occur in monazite with nine-fold coordination, while heavy rare earths concentrate in xenotime with eight-fold coordination. These coordination differences alter bond strengths and dissolution rates during acid or alkaline digestion. Monazite responds better to hot concentrated sulphuric acid, while xenotime requires more controlled conditions due to higher stability. Bastnäsite, dominated by light rare earths, releases fluorocarbonate components during calcination, which alters surface chemistry and improves leachability. These mineralogical attributes dictate pre-treatment choices, including roasting, caustic cracking, and selective decomposition.

Metallurgical reduction of rare earth halides demands reductants with strong affinity for chlorine or fluorine. Calcium, lithium, and magnesium remain common reductants due to favourable thermodynamic profiles. Reduction of heavier rare earths requires higher temperatures and improved mass transfer because the resulting metals exhibit lower vapour pressures and higher viscosity in molten form. These metals often absorb oxygen, nitrogen, and hydrogen if exposed even briefly to ambient conditions. This forces the use of vacuum induction furnaces, inert gas chambers, and specialised crucibles.

Production of rare earth alloys introduces further complexity due to interactions between 4f electrons and conduction electrons in metallic matrices. Intermetallic compounds such as $Nd_2Fe_{14}B$, $SmCo_5$, and Sm_2Co_{17} derive performance from anisotropic magnetic interactions that depend on precise control of stoichiometry and impurity levels. Minor deviations in oxygen or carbon content weaken magnetic alignment and reduce coercivity. This sensitivity arises from the delicate balance between 4f electron localisation and exchange interactions in the metal lattice.

Recycling processes depend on chemical characteristics at the elemental level. Permanent magnets contain tightly bound rare earths within metallic phases, which limits direct hydrometallurgical access. Selective hydrogen decrepitation breaks magnet structures at grain boundaries and exposes rare earth-rich domains without full dissolution. This process exploits hydrogen absorption behaviour that varies among lanthanides due to electronic configuration. Catalytic converters and phosphor powders require different strategies. Cerium and lanthanum oxides from catalysts resist simple leaching due to stable oxide phases, while europium and terbium phosphors require reducing agents and selective complexants to recover active components.

These chemical features shape every stage of the rare earth value chain, from geochemical concentration through processing and high-purity refinement to their integration into advanced alloys and devices. The behaviour of the 4f electron system defines their stability, reactivity, separation difficulty, and performance in strategic technologies.

1.2 Classification of light and heavy rare earth elements

Classification of rare earth elements into light and heavy groups reflects structural, electronic, and geochemical behaviour rather than simple atomic number sorting. Light rare earth elements extend from lanthanum through samarium. Their larger ionic radii produce lower charge density and weaker electrostatic attraction within oxide, phosphate, and carbonate lattices. This causes greater partitioning into early crystallising magmatic minerals and a stronger presence in primary ore minerals such as bastnäsite and monazite. Their wider ionic radii also influence hydration enthalpies, which remain less negative for these elements and create distinct trends in their solubility and complex stability in natural waters and industrial leach circuits. Light elements show reduced affinity for strong ligands such as fluoride and possess lower formation constants with organophosphorus extractants, which influences separation strategies in hydrometallurgical circuits.

Heavy rare earth elements run from gadolinium to lutetium and include yttrium due to its matching ionic radius in the trivalent state. These elements present the highest contraction effects within the series. Their smaller radii generate higher charge density and stronger electrostatic interaction with anions in solid-state matrices. This produces tighter lattice binding and increases resistance to acid digestion unless pre-treated through roasting or alkaline cracking. Heavy elements form more stable complexes with fluoride, sulphate, and chelating ligands. Their complexation behaviour drives strong adsorption onto clay minerals in subtropical weathering environments, leading to the development of ion-adsorption clay deposits. These deposits contain heavy rare earths in weakly bound states on clay surfaces, which makes salt leaching feasible without aggressive chemical digestion. Industrial systems value this behaviour because separation circuits for heavy elements rely on strong ligand interactions, rising distribution coefficients, and predictable extraction sequences.

The split between light and heavy groups also influences magnetic, optical, and electronic behaviour. Light elements possess lower magnetic anisotropy due to reduced 4f electron localisation. This gives them roles in catalytic processes and bulk alloys rather than high-performance magnetic structures. Heavy rare earths show strong spin orbit coupling and higher magnetocrystalline anisotropy, supporting their use in advanced permanent magnets where dysprosium and terbium stabilise coercivity at elevated temperatures. Optical transitions display systematic shifts across the classification. Light elements show more intense broad-band transitions, while heavy elements provide narrow emission lines that serve optical devices with strict spectral requirements.

Geochemical signatures strengthen the classification. Fractionation during magmatic differentiation, metamorphic mobilisation, and sedimentary processes follows predictable patterns due to the radius-controlled behaviour of the trivalent state. Light elements mobilise more readily in high-temperature fluids and partition strongly into carbonatites and alkalic magmas. Heavy elements concentrate preferentially in late-stage fluids or residual phases with tighter coordination sites, producing xenotime-rich domains with higher stability. This pattern supports exploration models because rare earth concentration zones follow distinct lithological, structural, and fluid pathways linked directly to this classification.

Industrial planning depends on this split. Light rare earths dominate global production volume because bastnäsite and monazite deposits contain them in high abundance. Heavy rare earth supply remains scarce due to limited ion-adsorption clay deposits and high extraction difficulty in refractory minerals. This scarcity influences pricing behaviour, geopolitical tensions, and long-term supply strategies. The classification is not a simple naming convention. It reflects precise chemical forces derived from the 4f orbital contraction, charge density gradients, ligand stability patterns, and coordinated mineralogical behaviour that govern extraction, refining, and strategic use.

Light rare earth elements display broader coordination environments in solid-state structures due to their larger ionic radii. Ninefold and even tenfold coordination sites in monazite and bastnäsite accept La^{3+}, Ce^{3+}, Pr^{3+}, Nd^{3+}, and Sm^{3+} with lower lattice strain. This behaviour controls dissolution kinetics during processing. Larger coordination polyhedra break more readily during acid sulphate decomposition and during alkaline cracking because bond strengths remain lower than those of the heavy end members. Thermodynamic data show less negative Gibbs free energies of hydration for light elements. This increases aqueous mobility in mildly acidic and bicarbonate-rich solutions. These trends explain why light rare earths appear enriched in carbonatitic systems, alkali intrusions, and volcanic-hydrothermal complexes where fluid pathways remain dominated by carbonate and chloride complexes. Light rare earth enrichment in these environments reflects weaker complex stability and greater sensitivity to temperature-driven solubility functions.

Heavy rare earth elements form more compact coordination environments due to high charge density and reduced ionic radii. Eightfold coordination becomes dominant in xenotime-type phosphates and various silicate structures. Strong electrostatic forces generate high bond dissociation energies, which increase resistance to both acid digestion and thermal decomposition. Heavy elements exhibit more negative hydration energies that stabilise strong inner-sphere complexes with sulphate, fluoride, phosphate, and organic chelators. This behaviour allows selective mobilisation in low pH, high ionic strength environments typical of subtropical lateritic systems. Clay adsorption complexes form through outer-sphere electrostatic forces and inner-sphere ligand exchange on kaolinite and halloysite surfaces. This binding remains reversible through ammonium salt leaching, which exploits cation exchange without attacking the mineral structure. This explains the industrial importance of ion-adsorption clay deposits for heavy rare earth supply.

The classification also reflects distinct behaviour under solvent extraction. Organic extractants based on phosphine oxides, phosphonic acids, and phosphinic acids display distribution coefficients that rise sharply across the lanthanide sequence. Heavy rare earths load preferentially into the organic phase due to stronger interaction between the extractant ligand and the highly charged cation. The resulting separation factors define commercial circuit design. Light rare earths require larger extraction volumes and more stages to achieve high purity, while heavy rare earths require fewer stages but produce lower throughput due to lower abundance. Separation processes must account for hydration shell differences because heavy rare earth ions lose tightly bound water molecules more readily during inner-sphere complex formation. This step increases extraction efficiency and improves kinetic performance in multi-stage circuits.

Magnetic and optical classification follows electronic structure. Light rare earths tend to show weaker magnetocrystalline anisotropy because 4f electron density extends less tightly around the nucleus. Heavy rare earths show stronger spin orbit coupling, which increases anisotropy and stabilises magnetic alignment under thermal load. This underpins industrial reliance on dysprosium and terbium for high-temperature magnet stability. Optical responses also diverge. Light rare earths display transitions influenced by higher energy 5d levels, which produce broader absorption bands. Heavy rare earths maintain tight f-f transitions with narrow emission lines because the 4f shell contracts and increases shielding stability. These patterns support optical filter production, medical imaging contrast systems, and high-precision laser components.

Pricing and supply dynamics reflect the classification. Light rare earths appear in higher concentrations in common ores, which leads to abundant supply and lower baseline costs. Heavy rare earths remain rare because geological systems only produce economic concentrations within specific climatic and geochemical niches. This scarcity factors into national stockpile strategies and off-take agreements that secure long-term supply for magnet production, military systems, and advanced electronics. Governments monitor heavy rare earth availability due to high substitutability limits and constrained refining capacity.

The division between light and heavy rare earth elements supports predictive modelling across geological, chemical, and industrial domains. Each group displays distinct trace element signatures that define exploration vectors. Light rare earth enrichment produces convex-up chondrite normalised profiles with smooth decreases from La to Sm. These signatures appear in carbonatites, peralkaline intrusions, and metasomatised mantle sources. They indicate fluid dominated transport systems with high carbonate activity. Geochemical dispersion halos around these systems contain light rare earth anomalies that extend through saprolite and colluvium due to higher solubility and weaker adsorption. Heavy rare earth enrichment produces concave profiles with elevated Gd, Tb, Dy, Ho, Er, Tm, Yb, and Lu values. These profiles link to xenotime rich pegmatites, high grade metamorphic terrains, and ion adsorption clays derived from granitic parent rocks. Anomalies remain localised because heavy elements bind strongly to clays and resist long range transport.

Thermodynamic modelling supports this classification. Activity coefficients, hydration numbers, and ligand stability constants follow clear radius controlled trends. Light elements show higher activity at moderate ionic strengths and maintain simpler aqueous speciation forms. Heavy elements require more complex models with strong ligand dependence. This difference affects equilibrium calculations in industrial circuits. Solvent extraction models incorporate stability constants, hydration energies, and partition functions that increase from light to heavy elements. Process engineers adjust acidity, ligand concentration, and phase contact time to exploit these gradients. Ion exchange modelling shows similar patterns because column displacement curves shift systematically across the series as heavy elements bind more strongly to resin sites.

The classification influences alloy design. Light rare earth metals integrate into steelmaking and non ferrous alloys as modifiers that alter grain structure, oxygen activity, and inclusion morphology. Their larger radii and lower electronegativity reduce localised lattice distortion and generate stable inclusions that refine grain size. Heavy rare earths integrate into intermetallic compounds where 4f electron localisation drives anisotropic magnetic behaviour. Dysprosium and terbium additions alter domain wall movement and coercivity in Nd Fe B magnets. These effects depend on site occupancy within the crystal lattice and the distribution of heavy elements within grain boundaries. This behaviour links directly to the contraction driven differences that separate light from heavy elements.

Environmental behaviour follows the same classification. Light elements show increased mobility during acid mine drainage because less negative hydration energies and lower complex stability allow faster dissolution from host minerals. Heavy elements show slower release rates but stronger adsorption onto clay and organic matter. This requires different remediation strategies. Light element rich waters need pH control and lime treatment to precipitate carbonates and hydroxides. Heavy element contamination requires selective ion exchange or sorption processes because heavy rare earth ions remain stable in complexed forms that resist simple precipitation.

Economic models use the classification to assess project feasibility. Deposits dominated by light rare earths rely on high ore grades and large tonnages to remain competitive due to lower prices and high supply. Heavy rare earth projects rely on small tonnage but high value because heavy elements supply strategic industries such as electric motors, defence systems, and optical technologies. Risk models show stronger price volatility for heavy elements because limited producers, long permitting times, and narrow geological availability constrain supply elasticity.

The classification defines the structural logic of the rare earth sector. Light and heavy elements follow separate geochemical pathways, exhibit distinct ligand chemistry, and drive different industrial applications. Their differences shape global supply chains, influence extraction technology, and define long term strategic planning for governments and industry.

1.3 Misconceptions about scarcity
Public debate often misinterprets rare earth scarcity because the term rare suggests geological shortage, yet the crustal abundance profile shows values comparable to copper, zinc, and nickel. The misconception arises from the difference between total crustal abundance and economically recoverable concentration. Rare earth elements disperse widely in primary igneous and sedimentary systems, yet seldom accumulate in grades high enough to support commercial extraction. Their lithophile behaviour drives broad distribution across silicates, phosphates, and carbonates where they form trace components locked within resistant crystal lattices. This distribution pattern reduces ore grade without reducing total quantity. Most crustal material contains rare earths in the hundred parts per million range, yet commercial extraction requires grades far above this threshold due to energy demand, reagent consumption, and waste generation during beneficiation.

Scarcity myths also emerge from limited refining capacity rather than geological shortage. Production bottlenecks occur in the separation stage where chemically similar trivalent ions require extensive multi stage solvent extraction circuits. These circuits demand large quantities of organic extractants, diluents, and acid streams, which restrict global capacity due to environmental regulation, operating cost, and technical complexity. Nations with limited refining infrastructure rely on a small number of producers that maintain large separation plants. This concentration fosters the false impression that rare earths themselves are scarce when the actual constraint lies within processing throughput rather than mineral occurrence.

Deposit type distribution reinforces the misconception. Light rare earth enriched carbonatites such as Bayan Obo and Mountain Pass contain large reserves, yet heavy rare earth enriched ion adsorption clays dominate only in select climatic and geological regimes. Low temperatures, specific weathering intensity, and granitic parent rocks create these deposits. Their formation requires long term leaching that removes major cations and leaves rare earth ions bound to clay surfaces through reversible electrostatic interactions. This process does not occur widely, which gives a misleading perception that heavy rare earths face geological shortage. The constraint originates from formation conditions, not absolute crustal abundance. Heavy elements concentrate in residual phases and accessory minerals such as xenotime, which exist in many terrains but in refractory mineral forms that resist economical extraction.

Market narratives further amplify scarcity myths because price spikes follow geopolitical events, export restrictions, or regulatory changes in producing nations. These spikes mislead observers into assuming geological depletion. Analysts without metallurgical background often equate price volatility with diminishing reserves even when proven and probable resources remain large. Price behaviour reflects supply chain concentration, refining constraints, and demand surges from magnet, catalyst, or battery sectors. It does not reflect absolute quantity in the crust.

The misconception also persists due to confusion between rare earth oxides and high purity separated rare earth metals. Oxide concentrates remain abundant, yet high purity metals require long separation chains and strict process controls. High purity dysprosium, terbium, and europium require extensive extraction cycles because minute differences in ionic radius govern separation. These steps generate limited throughput and high cost. Observers often interpret the high price of high purity output as a sign of geological rarity, yet the constraint lies in the difficulty of chemical separation. This distinction remains central to understanding scarcity and remains absent in many policy debates.

Misconceptions persist because observers conflate reserve estimates with static geological facts, yet reserve classifications depend on economic, regulatory, and technological parameters that shift over time. Rare earth reserves expand when extraction methods improve, separation efficiency increases, reagent costs fall, or market prices rise enough to justify investment. Declared reserves contract when environmental compliance costs increase or when extraction technology fails to meet regulatory thresholds. These changes occur independently of actual crustal endowment. Policymakers often overlook this dynamic behaviour and treat reserves as fixed quantities, which distorts assessments of long term supply security. The classification of resources into measured, indicated, and inferred categories also contributes to misunderstanding. Rare earth mineralisation frequently remains under drilled because exploration companies prioritise metals with shorter permitting cycles. This produces data scarcity, not geological scarcity.

Another misconception arises from the complex mineralogy that hosts rare earths. Elements occur in a wide range of minerals, including bastnäsite, monazite, xenotime, synchysite, parisite, allanite, eudialyte, apatite, and zircon. The presence of rare earths in these minerals does not guarantee economic extraction because each mineral has its own thermal stability, chemical resistance, and response to acids or alkalis. Hard rock deposits often contain refractory minerals that require aggressive pre treatment. Without these steps, dissolution rates remain too low to support commercial processing. This gives the appearance of scarcity when the underlying issue is chemical complexity. Refractory minerals hold large amounts of rare earths, yet the cost of accessing them exceeds market value under current technology. Shifts in leaching chemistry, roasting strategies, or selective reagents can convert previously uneconomic material into recoverable reserves.

Processing difficulty also fuels the false perception of scarcity. Beneficiation stages often struggle to separate rare earth rich minerals from gangue due to fine grain size, intergrowths, and similar surface properties. Flotation performance varies with pH control, collector type, and surface activation. Magnetic separation yields limited selectivity because only minor variations exist in magnetic susceptibility across many rare earth bearing minerals. These limitations produce low recovery rates in some deposits, which leads investors to assume that the rare earth content itself is insufficient. The barrier originates from processing inefficiency rather than geological depletion.

Environmental regulation contributes to the misconception. Rare earth bearing minerals often contain thorium and uranium as lattice bound impurities. Safe handling, waste management, and long term disposal add operational cost and regulatory complexity. Many jurisdictions restrict development of monazite rich deposits due to radiological concerns rather than lack of material. Deposits remain unexploited because regulatory compliance outweighs economic return. This stagnation reinforces the false idea that the planet lacks rare earth resources when the issue reflects regulatory conditions instead of natural scarcity.

Demand concentration in specific high value elements also distorts perception. Neodymium, praseodymium, dysprosium, and terbium face strong industrial demand due to their role in magnets for electric motors and wind turbines. These four elements represent a small fraction of total crustal rare earth content, yet they dominate industrial value. Observers often generalise shortages of these elements to the entire rare earth family. Light rare earths such as lanthanum and cerium remain abundant and often oversupplied relative to demand. Oversupply leads to stock accumulation, which contradicts the narrative of geological scarcity. Misinterpretation occurs when market signals from one subset of the group are projected onto all rare earths.

Misconceptions about scarcity intensify because observers focus on mine output rather than the global pipeline of undeveloped projects. Dozens of carbonatite, alkaline, lateritic, placer, and pegmatite deposits remain at pre-feasibility stages. These projects contain large tonnages across both light and heavy rare earth groups, yet remain idle due to long permitting cycles, high separation costs, and market uncertainty. Mine development timelines extend beyond ten years because environmental impact assessments, community agreements, radiological approvals, and infrastructure requirements impose multiple sequential bottlenecks. This delay produces a supply gap that has nothing to do with geological depletion. Public discourse often interprets this gap as material scarcity rather than a function of project maturation and capital deployment.

Another persistent misconception links scarcity to export controls. When producing countries introduce quotas, tariffs, or licence restrictions, market participants often assume depletion or reduced ore grades. Export policy usually reflects strategic planning, environmental compliance, or efforts to consolidate domestic refining. These measures influence the flow of separated oxides, metals, and alloys, not the amount of rare earth elements available in the crust. Observers unfamiliar with mining economics often equate export limits with geological shortage, yet the relationship does not exist. Export restrictions manipulate supply chain behaviour and pricing but leave global reserves untouched.

Misunderstanding grows further due to low public awareness of recycling potential. End of life magnets, phosphor powders, nickel metal hydride batteries, and catalyst materials contain high concentrations of rare earths with purity levels that reduce separation complexity. Recycling streams remain technically viable, yet adoption progresses slowly because supply chains lack collection networks, sorting infrastructure, and stable policy incentives. Policymakers often misjudge recycling as marginal due to limited current output. The issue reflects system design, not material scarcity. Large resource volumes exist within urban mines, yet remain underutilised. Once collection scales, recycled rare earths will offset primary supply, further disproving scarcity narratives.

Another source of confusion stems from the difference between accessible deposits and operational competitiveness. Many known deposits sit in remote regions with insufficient infrastructure, limited water supply, or energy constraints. High logistics cost reduces economic viability and delays development. These constraints mirror broader resource sector challenges rather than rare earth specific scarcity. Projects in Arctic regions, deep inland deserts, or politically unstable jurisdictions remain undeveloped due to risk, cost, and governance issues. Public perception often interprets these undeveloped resources as evidence of geological shortage, yet the underlying cause remains logistical and financial.

Misconceptions also appear in technological discussions. High purity separated products such as dysprosium metal, terbium oxide, and europium oxide require extensive solvent extraction sequences with hundreds of contact stages. This slow production rate gives the impression of limited physical availability. Observers often misinterpret long production lead times as proof of geological absence. The constraint arises from the subtle chemical differences within the lanthanide group. Separation plants must run through numerous iterations to isolate each element. Output rates remain slow not because sources lack material, but because the chemistry requires lengthy, resource intensive processes.

Market biases reinforce scarcity myths because corporate communications, investment reports, and media narratives often emphasise shortage risk to justify project financing. Analysts amplify these messages and create a feedback loop that shapes public perception. Geological surveys and academic literature contradict these narratives by documenting large unexploited deposits across multiple continents. The gap between geological knowledge and market narratives sustains the scarcity misunderstanding.

Understanding these misconceptions remains essential for designing policy, supply strategies, and investment frameworks. Scarcity arises from processing capacity, regulatory constraints, market concentration, and technological challenges. It does not arise from lack of crustal material.

1.4 Historical development of rare earth mining
The development of rare earth mining began as a sequence of mineralogical discoveries rather than a coordinated industrial effort. Early observations in the late eighteenth century identified unusual

oxides within heavy minerals extracted from quarries and pegmatites in Scandinavia. Chemists isolated these oxides through repeated precipitation, calcination, and fractional crystallisation. The slow pace reflected the difficulty of separating trivalent ions with nearly identical radii and charge densities. Analytical chemistry of the period lacked tools to discriminate between individual lanthanides, which slowed classification. Mineralogical mapping during the nineteenth century revealed that granites, syenites, and carbonatites hosted lanthanide bearing minerals such as monazite, xenotime, and bastnäsite. These discoveries established the geological framework that underlies modern exploration. Early miners extracted monazite from placer sands because mechanical separation proved feasible with basic gravity circuits. This marked the first scalable extraction route and supplied thorium and rare earths for incandescent gas mantles and early lighting systems.

Industrial interest accelerated in the early twentieth century as chemical industries sought stable catalysts, polishing powders, and alloy additives. Monazite sands from India, Brazil, and the United States supported these markets because placer deposits delivered high concentration minerals without complex beneficiation. Chemical plants used hot concentrated sulphuric acid digestion followed by selective precipitation to isolate individual rare earth fractions. This process left thorium rich residues that required secure storage but provided stable revenue streams for companies focused on early lighting technologies. Rare earth mining remained limited in scale, yet the chemical sector gained experience with acid digestion, solvent extraction precursors, and redox manipulation. These industrial practices set the baseline for later hydrometallurgical methods.

Exploration and mining changed in the mid twentieth century with the identification of extensive carbonatite systems containing bastnäsite and monazite in primary ore bodies rather than alluvial environments. Carbonatite complexes in the United States and China revealed rare earth concentrations high enough to justify open pit mining, flotation, roasting, and solvent extraction. Mountain Pass emerged as one of the first large scale integrated rare earth mines. It used bastnäsite flotation followed by roasting to remove fluorocarbonate groups and improve leachability. The operation supplied lanthanum and cerium for catalysts and polishing powders. It also produced neodymium and praseodymium for early magnet research. This marked a shift from small batch chemistry to industrial scale production with continuous circuits and expanding refinery capacity.

China's development of rare earth mining during the late twentieth century reshaped the sector. Exploration across Inner Mongolia identified massive bastnäsite dominant ore at Bayan Obo. This deposit contained both light rare earths and iron resources, facilitating integrated mining operations and high throughput beneficiation. Simultaneously, research teams in southern China identified ion adsorption clays rich in heavy rare earths. These clays responded to salt leaching at ambient temperature, which allowed extraction without roasting or strong acids. China invested in large solvent extraction facilities capable of separating all lanthanides at commercial scale. These plants introduced extensive mixer settler trains, high capacity organic solvents, and precise pH control circuits. The combination of abundant feedstock, low processing costs, and state supported infrastructure established China as the global leader in rare earth separation and shaped the modern supply chain.

The expansion of rare earth mining during the late twentieth and early twenty first century followed demand growth in magnets, phosphors, and catalytic converters. The rise of Nd Fe B magnets for electric motors and hard drives created sustained demand for neodymium, praseodymium, dysprosium, and terbium. Mining companies explored hard rock and clay deposits in Australia, Africa, North America, and Southeast Asia. Lynas developed the Mount Weld deposit with high grade light rare earths and built separation capacity in Malaysia. Renewed interest in monazite rich heavy mineral sands revived projects in Africa and India, although regulatory concerns over thorium slowed expansion.

These developments show that historical trends reflect shifts in technology, demand, and policy rather than geological scarcity. Early work focused on placer sands due to simple beneficiation. Later phases targeted carbonatites for high grade, high tonnage ore. Ion adsorption clays opened access to heavy rare earths that previously remained locked in refractory minerals. Each phase advanced processing methods, from sulphuric acid digestion to advanced solvent extraction and adsorption based leaching. Rare earth mining evolved from laboratory isolation to a complex global supply chain integrated with metallurgy, logistics, energy policy, and strategic planning.

The historical trajectory of rare earth mining shifted further during the 1980s and 1990s as global industries required higher purity products for electronics, fibre optics, and precision devices. Applications in colour televisions, fluorescent lighting, laser systems, and advanced ceramics demanded strict control of impurity levels, oxidation states, and particle morphology. These requirements drove major improvements in solvent extraction design. Engineers increased the number of mixer settler stages, introduced counter current configurations, and deployed phosphonic and phosphinic acid extractants with higher separation factors. These innovations allowed producers to isolate each lanthanide at commercial scale with consistent purity. This technical leap elevated the role of separation plants and positioned refining capacity as the core constraint in the global supply chain. Mining no longer represented the dominant cost or barrier. Separation chemistry became the critical limiting step.

China scaled extraction and refining simultaneously. Bayan Obo's integration with steel operations delivered cost advantages through shared infrastructure, transport networks, and power supply. State supported research institutes focused on extractant formulation, process modelling, and control systems that stabilised continuous operation across hundreds of extraction stages. Ion adsorption clays in the south offered a complementary source of heavy rare earths, giving China a complete portfolio of light and heavy elements. Leaching teams optimised ammonium sulphate solutions, pH windows, and column leaching strategies that minimised clay disturbance while maximising rare earth desorption. This supported low cost extraction without roasting or high temperature processing. These developments produced a structural shift where China supplied the majority of global separated rare earth oxides, metals, and alloys.

Global producers struggled to compete because environmental standards in many jurisdictions restricted acid discharge, tailings storage, and radioactive residue handling. Monazite rich deposits carried thorium levels that triggered strict radiological controls. These controls increased capital costs for tailings dams, encapsulation systems, and long term monitoring. Companies faced rising compliance costs that reduced competitiveness relative to China's integrated operations. This created a perception of global scarcity even though geological resources remained abundant. The bottleneck reflected regulatory divergence and geopolitical risk rather than depletion.

During the 2000s, demand for Nd Fe B magnets accelerated due to hybrid vehicles, wind turbines, and digital storage. This prompted renewed exploration across Africa, North America, and Australia. Projects such as Mount Weld, Nolans Bore, Strange Lake, and Nechalacho advanced through feasibility stages. Each deposit faced distinct processing challenges due to mineralogical complexity. Eudialyte dominant deposits required chloride leaching and careful silica management. Allanite rich ores required higher energy grinding and selective flotation with tailored collectors. These challenges delayed development and created long lead times for new supply. Investors interpreted the delay as geological shortage, although the underlying cause remained technological.

The Fukushima accident in 2011 increased scrutiny on radioactive waste from monazite and xenotime processing. Several countries tightened regulatory frameworks. Companies with monazite feedstocks faced stricter permits and waste disposal obligations, which increased processing cost and reduced global output. This reinforced the misleading impression that rare earths were scarce. Meanwhile, China enforced tighter environmental regulations within its own borders, restructuring illegal and informal operations and consolidating supply under state owned enterprises. This consolidation reduced exports temporarily, which triggered price spikes and intensified the scarcity narrative in international markets.

These industrial and regulatory phases show that historical fluctuations in supply originated from changing technology, refining capacity, energy cost, environmental rules, and geopolitical strategy. Geological inventory remained large and stable. The apparent scarcity reflected the structure of the supply chain rather than the amount of material in the crust.

The most recent phase in the development of rare earth mining reflects the interaction between energy transition policy, strategic competition, and advances in digital exploration. Electric vehicles, offshore wind turbines, and high efficiency motors increased demand for neodymium, praseodymium, dysprosium, and terbium. Governments classified rare earths as strategic minerals and introduced incentives for domestic extraction and refining. This shifted investment patterns toward early stage projects that previously lacked financing. Geological surveys expanded datasets of carbonatite complexes, alkaline intrusions, and peralkaline systems through airborne geophysics, remote sensing, and high resolution geochemical mapping. Machine learning algorithms improved targeting by integrating magnetic data, radiometric signatures, and lithological models. These tools increased discovery rates and confirmed that geological availability exceeded previous estimates.

Processing innovation followed. Researchers improved roasting strategies for monazite and bastnäsite by integrating controlled atmosphere calcination, selective phase decomposition, and temperature programmed leaching. These steps reduced reagent consumption and increased leach efficiency. Ion exchange resins with functionalised ligands improved separation of heavy rare earths from chloride and nitrate media. Membrane systems with nanoporous structures allowed selective passage of lanthanide complexes based on charge density and hydration structure. These methods remain early in adoption but indicate a shift toward reduced chemical intensity and improved selectivity compared to conventional solvent extraction.

Recycling emerged as a parallel development. Permanent magnets in electric motors, generators, and electronic devices contain high concentrations of neodymium, praseodymium, dysprosium, and terbium. Hydrogen decrepitation produced friable powder that exposed rare earth rich domains for hydrometallurgical recovery. Thermal demagnetisation and selective acid leaching improved extraction from end of life products. Phosphor powders, catalysts, and nickel metal hydride batteries formed additional recycling streams. These technologies created secondary supply sources with consistent chemistry and reduced mineralogical complexity compared to primary ores. This expansion undermined scarcity narratives and reduced reliance on newly mined feedstock.

International supply chain restructuring formed another major step in the historical development. The United States established programmes to rebuild separation capacity and secure heavy rare earth supply chains. Europe launched initiatives to develop domestic refining, recycling, and magnet manufacturing. Japan expanded partnerships with Australia and Vietnam to diversify feedstocks. These policies focused on risk management rather than geological constraints. New separation plants in Australia and the United States introduced modular mixer settler designs, improved organic phase stability, and advanced process control systems. These changes improved separation efficiency, reduced solvent losses, and lowered waste generation.

Meanwhile, ion adsorption clay extraction evolved toward more regulated and environmentally controlled methods. Operators reduced ammonium discharge, introduced closed loop leaching systems, and implemented column leaching to minimise land disturbance. These improvements addressed environmental impacts and stabilised supply of heavy rare earths. The industry shifted from small scale artisanal operations to structured, monitored extraction supported by state enterprises and regulated contractors.

The historical development of rare earth mining shows a progression shaped by scientific discovery, chemical innovation, environmental policy, and strategic planning. Each stage expanded the industry's technical capacity and revealed new sources of material. None of these stages reflected geological depletion. The evolution of mining and refining focused on overcoming chemical similarity, mineralogical complexity, and regulatory constraints. The modern rare earth sector now integrates geology, metallurgy, environmental engineering, and geopolitics into a single framework that defines how deposits move from discovery to market ready products.

2. Geological Formation and Global Distribution

2.1 Mineralogical occurrence and typical host rocks

Rare earth elements occur within a wide spectrum of primary and secondary minerals that form under specific geochemical and petrological conditions. Their lithophile nature drives incorporation into silicate, phosphate, carbonate, and fluoride bearing phases during magmatic and hydrothermal processes. The most common primary host minerals include bastnäsite, monazite, xenotime, apatite, allanite, synchysite, parisite, eudialyte, and fluorocarbonates. Each mineral records a distinct crystallographic environment, ionic radius preference, and oxidation sensitivity that governs rare earth distribution at the deposit scale.

Bastnäsite dominates in carbonatite and alkaline systems. Its fluorocarbonate structure accommodates light rare earths through ninefold coordination. The mineral forms in magmatic or hydrothermal environments where fluorine rich fluids stabilise carbonate complexation. Bastnäsite remains common in systems with high CO_2 activity and low silica saturation, which produce alkaline-carbonatite complexes with long lived intrusive histories. Grain size varies from coarse magmatic crystals to fine hydrothermal aggregates. These textures influence flotation performance and dictate beneficiation strategy.

Monazite, a phosphate mineral, hosts light rare earths with thorium substitution driven by charge balance mechanisms. It forms in peraluminous granites, pegmatites, and high grade metamorphic terrains. Monazite resists weathering due to high lattice energy and survives sediment transport. This produces placer concentrations in coastal and fluvial settings where heavy mineral sands accumulate. Monazite persists in these environments due to mechanical stability and density contrast with quartz and feldspar. Its phosphate structure increases resistance to acid attack, requiring roasting or intensive sulphuric acid digestion during processing.

Xenotime, a yttrium phosphate, hosts heavy rare earths within tight eightfold coordination sites. It forms in granitic pegmatites, high grade metamorphic belts, and hydrothermal veins where phosphate rich fluids interact with aluminous lithologies. Xenotime also survives mechanical weathering and accumulates in placer deposits. Its crystal chemistry drives strong partitioning of heavy rare earths, which produces concentrated, high value mineral domains. Xenotime's high lattice energy increases chemical resistance and influences processing cost.

Allanite, an epidote group silicate, contains variable amounts of rare earths within a complex lattice. It forms in granitoids, metamorphic rocks, and volcanic systems. Allanite often hosts cerium, lanthanum, and neodymium but remains chemically unstable under weathering. It breaks down into secondary clays and iron oxides, releasing rare earths into soils. Weathering profiles derived from allanite bearing lithologies contribute to the formation of ion adsorption clays that hold heavy rare earths through surface adsorption rather than crystal lattice incorporation.

Eudialyte, a zirconium silicate found in peralkaline systems, contains rare earths as minor lattice constituents. It forms in agpaitic nepheline syenites where high alkali content stabilises complex silicate structures. Eudialyte displays fine grained intergrowths that complicate beneficiation. Its breakdown during processing releases silica rich gels that interfere with leaching circuits. These mineralogical constraints limit large scale exploitation despite high rare earth grades.

Carbonatite complexes represent the most significant host rocks for primary rare earth enrichment. They consist of intrusive or extrusive carbonate rich magmas derived from mantle sources with high volatile content. Carbonatites often show zoned mineralisation with bastnäsite, monazite, fluorite, barite, iron oxides, and apatite. Their association with fenite alteration halos provides exploration markers. Alkaline igneous complexes such as syenites, ijolites, nepheline syenites, and peralkaline granites also host rare earth minerals due to incompatible element enrichment during late stage magmatic differentiation.

Ion adsorption clays form in subtropical regions where prolonged weathering of granitic and rhyolitic lithologies releases rare earths into soil profiles. Clay minerals such as kaolinite and halloysite adsorb trivalent ions by outer sphere complexation. These deposits concentrate heavy rare earths and yttrium due to stronger adsorption affinity and lower mobility. Their genesis depends on climate, parent rock chemistry, and leaching intensity rather than high initial ore grade.

These mineralogical and geological environments form the foundation of rare earth exploration. Mineral stability, grain size, coordination geometry, and host rock chemistry govern extractive potential and processing requirements. Each deposit reflects the interaction between primary magmatic processes and secondary weathering that controls the distribution of rare earths within the crust.

Mineralogical occurrence of rare earth elements reflects crystallographic controls governed by ionic radius, charge density, and structural compatibility within host lattices. Light rare earths occupy larger coordination sites and tend to form minerals with ninefold or higher coordination, while heavy rare earths occupy more compact sites in eightfold coordination structures. These structural preferences dictate mineral assemblages across different geological environments.

Carbonatite hosted systems illustrate this behaviour clearly. Magmatic carbonatites crystallise from CO_2 rich, low silica melts that concentrate incompatible elements, including rare earths. Bastnäsite forms during late magmatic or early hydrothermal stages where fluorine activity allows stabilisation of fluorocarbonate complexes. Monazite and synchysite also appear in these systems, often associated with barite, fluorite, calcite, ankerite, and magnetite. Rare earths partition strongly into the carbonate melt due to low solubility in coexisting silicate phases. This partitioning enriches rare earth content in central intrusive zones, dykes, and late stage veins. Fenite alteration zones around carbonatite intrusions supply geochemical targets due to alkali metasomatism that re mobilises rare earths and related incompatible elements.

Alkaline and peralkaline igneous systems provide another major host environment. These rocks undergo extensive fractional crystallisation due to their high alkali content, producing strong enrichment of incompatible elements during late differentiation. Eudialyte, rinkite, mosandrite, loparite, pyrochlore, and apatite often host rare earths within these systems. Rare earths partition into late stage residual fluids that form pegmatitic or hydrothermal veins rich in complex silicate, titanate, and phosphate minerals. Mineral textures range from coarse interlocking crystals to fine microcrystalline intergrowths that challenge beneficiation. The stability of these minerals depends on their structural complexity, and their breakdown may produce gels or colloidal material during processing.

Granite related rare earth occurrences include monazite, xenotime, allanite, and zircon. These minerals form during fractional crystallisation of felsic magmas where rare earths behave as incompatible components. Monazite crystallises in peraluminous granites where phosphorus levels support phosphate mineral growth. Xenotime forms where yttrium and heavy rare earths reach sufficient concentration during late stage crystallisation. Allanite forms in more calc alkaline granites and hosts light rare earths through coupled substitution mechanisms involving iron and aluminium. Zircon incorporates rare earths in trace amounts but serves as an indicator mineral during exploration due to its resistance to alteration and robust trace element signature.

Metamorphic environments generate rare earth bearing minerals through recrystallisation and reaction textures. High grade metamorphism produces monazite growth in pelitic rocks through breakdown of apatite and allanite. Xenotime grows during metamorphism of aluminous rocks and often records deformation history. These minerals trap rare earths in tightly bonded structures with high geochemical stability. Their presence supports exploration in metamorphic terrains where primary igneous signatures have been overprinted.

Hydrothermal systems transport rare earths through chloride, carbonate, and fluoride complexes. These fluids precipitate rare earth minerals when temperature, pH, and ligand concentration shift during fluid rock interaction. Hydrothermal bastnäsite, parisite, synchysite, and fluorite rich assemblages form in veins and breccias near carbonatite or alkaline intrusive complexes. These veins represent secondary enrichment zones that increase grade locally. Fluid inclusion studies show that rare earth transport occurs at moderate temperatures and involves CO_2 rich, saline solutions with variable pH.

Ion adsorption clays represent secondary accumulations formed through prolonged weathering. Primary minerals such as allanite, apatite, monazite, and zircon release rare earths during chemical weathering. Clay minerals bind trivalent ions through outer sphere electrostatic interaction and inner sphere ligand exchange at hydroxyl sites. Heavy rare earths show stronger adsorption due to higher charge density. These deposits occur in granitic terrains exposed to warm, humid climates that drive intense leaching. Soil profiles often show vertical zoning with heavy rare earth enrichment near the lower horizons where clay content increases.

The diversity of mineral hosts and geological settings demonstrates that rare earth occurrence depends on broad geochemical pathways rather than isolated mineral types. Host rock chemistry, fluid composition, thermal history, and weathering intensity define mineral assemblages and control extraction complexity.

The distribution of rare earth minerals within host rocks reflects precise geochemical controls that operate during magma evolution, fluid migration, and surface alteration. These controls define how elements partition among crystallising phases and how they concentrate into ore forming systems. Rare earths behave as incompatible elements in most magmatic regimes. Their ionic radii and trivalent charge prevent incorporation into major rock forming silicates such as olivine, pyroxene, amphibole, and feldspar. These phases lack coordination sites of appropriate size or charge balance. This exclusion drives enrichment in late stage melts and fluids where mineral assemblages shift toward carbonate, phosphate, and fluoride rich phases.

Carbonatite complexes represent the strongest concentration mechanism. They arise from mantle derived magmas rich in CO_2 and incompatible elements. Fractional crystallisation, immiscibility between silicate and carbonate melts, and repeated intrusive pulses create zones with extreme enrichment of light rare earths. Host rocks show textures ranging from coarse carbonatite cores to breccia pipes, dykes, and disseminated mineralisation in fenitised country rock. Bastnäsite dominates primary ore due to high fluorine activity. Monazite and parisite appear in late stage fluids. High temperature hydrothermal fluids re mobilise rare earths and produce vein and dissemination patterns within altered carbonatite and adjacent fenites. These systems show consistent mineralogical zoning that guides exploration drilling.

Peralkaline igneous complexes form another important environment. Their high alkali content stabilises unusual silicate, titanate, and zirconium rich minerals capable of hosting rare earths. Eudialyte bearing nepheline syenites from regions such as Greenland and Russia contain significant rare earth concentrations, yet mineral processing remains difficult due to reactive silica liberation during leaching. These host rocks show layered intrusions, pegmatitic zones, and late stage hydrothermal veins with fluorine rich mineral assemblages. Their petrological evolution often includes prolonged fractional crystallisation, which drives incompatible element enrichment toward late stage units. Rare earth minerals display intergrowths with alkali silicates that complicate liberation during comminution.

Granite related deposits depend on phosphorus availability and melt composition. Peraluminous granites crystallise monazite through reaction of phosphorus bearing melts with aluminous components. Xenotime crystallises when yttrium and heavy rare earths reach saturation levels in late differentiates. Associated pegmatites show coarse crystals of monazite, xenotime, and allanite. Rare earths also appear in accessory phases such as zircon, titanite, and apatite, where they substitute for major cations. These rocks resist alteration, so rare earths often remain locked within robust minerals unless subjected to intense weathering.

Metamorphic terrains modify primary rare earth mineralogy through recrystallisation, neoblast formation, and partial melting. Monazite inclusions in garnet, biotite, and sillimanite rich schists record metamorphic grade and deformation. Xenotime forms during high temperature, high pressure reactions involving aluminous protoliths. Metamorphic fluids re distribute rare earths over short distances, producing veinlets, small disseminations, or overgrowths on pre existing grains. These systems seldom create large ore bodies but provide exploration indicators.

Weathering generates secondary deposits through prolonged leaching. Ion adsorption clays hold rare earths through weak electrostatic interaction rather than lattice incorporation. Clay minerals with high surface area provide abundant hydroxyl sites that bind trivalent ions. Heavy rare earths dominate due to stronger adsorption. These deposits require granitic parent rocks rich in allanite, apatite, monazite, and zircon. Climate must remain warm and humid to sustain deep weathering profiles. Soil horizons show vertical differentiation, with upper layers depleted by leaching and lower layers enriched as rare earths accumulate on clay surfaces. These deposits represent a unique mineralogical environment with distinct extraction chemistry.

Sedimentary systems contribute additional concentrations through placer formation. Monazite and xenotime resist chemical and mechanical weathering, so they accumulate in heavy mineral sands. These sands form in coastal environments, beach placers, and river channels. Sorting processes driven by wave action, longshore currents, and fluvial transport concentrate dense minerals. Placer deposits remain economically significant for light and heavy rare earths along with titanium, zirconium, and tin.

Each host environment presents different mineralogical challenges. Carbonatites and peralkaline rocks provide high grade primary ore but require advanced flotation and roasting. Granite related minerals resist chemical attack and demand aggressive digestion. Ion adsorption clays allow simple leaching but occur in limited climatic zones. Placers provide stable feedstocks but require stringent radiological controls. The diversity of mineral hosts and rock types defines the global distribution of rare earth resources and determines extraction strategies across jurisdictions.

2.2 Major global deposits
Global rare earth production relies on a concentrated group of large deposits that combine favourable geology, scale, and established processing routes. These systems include carbonatites, ion adsorption clays, alkaline complexes, and heavy mineral sands. Each deposit presents specific mineralogical features, grade profiles, and

metallurgical challenges that define its position within the global supply chain.

Bayan Obo in Inner Mongolia represents the largest known rare earth deposit. It is a giant iron niobium rare earth system hosted within a carbonate altered dolomite sequence intruded by carbonatite dykes. Ore occurs in massive magnetite rich bodies, disseminations, and breccia zones. Bastnäsite and monazite dominate mineralogy. Grades range from two to six percent total rare earth oxides in the main ore zones. The scale of the deposit supports sustained mining through large open pit operations. High throughput flotation circuits concentrate rare earth minerals before acid roasting and solvent extraction. Bayan Obo provides most global light rare earth supply due to its size, strong infrastructure, and integrated refining capacity.

Mountain Pass in the United States remains the most significant rare earth system outside Asia. It consists of a carbonatite body rich in bastnäsite with low levels of radioactive impurities. The deposit formed through fractional crystallisation of a calcic carbonatite magma. It displays high neodymium and praseodymium content relative to many other light rare earth deposits. Early exploitation relied on bastnäsite flotation and calcination to remove CO_2 and fluorine species. Modern operations apply improved flotation reagents and updated hydrometallurgy to reduce waste and increase recovery. Mountain Pass provides a major source of light rare earths, although it lacks the heavy rare earth profile found in ion adsorption clays.

Mount Weld in Australia provides one of the highest grade rare earth deposits globally. It is a deeply weathered carbonatite pipe with primary bastnäsite and secondary phosphates enriched through prolonged tropical weathering. Ore grades exceed eight percent total rare earth oxides in some zones. The weathered profile increases mineral liberation and improves leaching efficiency. Light rare earths dominate, although minor heavy rare earth zones occur in deeper unweathered material. The deposit supplies ore for refining facilities in Malaysia. Its unusually high grade, thick weathered zones, and stable mineralogy support long term production planning.

Ion adsorption clay deposits in southern China form the primary source of heavy rare earths. These deposits occur in subtropical regions where prolonged weathering of granitic and rhyolitic parent rocks releases rare earths into clay rich soil profiles. Heavy rare earth elements such as yttrium, dysprosium, terbium, and erbium dominate because they bind strongly to clay surfaces through electrostatic interactions. Grades remain low at around one tenth of a percent total rare earth oxides, yet extraction requires simple salt leaching rather than complex mineral processing. This operational simplicity, combined with high value heavy rare earth elements, makes these deposits globally significant. Their limited geographic distribution constrains supply and influences strategic policy.

Lynas' Mount Weld project, the Dubbo zirconia and rare earth project in Australia, and the Nolans Bore deposit in the Northern Territory represent major new sources under development. These deposits contain combinations of bastnäsite, monazite, xenotime, and apatite within alkaline and carbonatite systems. They provide diversified light and middle rare earth profiles, although heavy rare earth concentrations remain moderate. Complex mineralogy increases processing difficulty, requiring multi step hydrometallurgical circuits.

Greenland hosts significant resources in the Kvanefjeld and Kringlerne deposits within large peralkaline intrusive complexes. Eudialyte dominates as the main mineral host. These deposits contain large tonnages with moderate grades but face metallurgical challenges due to silica gel formation during leaching. Their strategic importance lies in geographical diversification and potential long term supply.

African rare earth deposits include monazite rich heavy mineral sands in Madagascar, South Africa, Tanzania, and Mozambique. These coastal placer systems contain ilmenite, rutile, zircon, and monazite. They provide stable feedstocks with manageable mineralogy but require radiological controls due to thorium content. Hard rock deposits such as Ngualla in Tanzania and Steenkampskraal in South Africa offer additional sources with a mix of bastnäsite, monazite, and xenotime. These systems support both light and heavy rare earth production depending on mineral assemblage.

This network of global deposits underpins current and future rare earth supply. Each system reflects geological processes that concentrate rare earth elements into extractable volumes, yet each also presents distinct metallurgical and regulatory requirements. Their combined output defines the structure of the global market.

The global distribution of major rare earth deposits reflects specific petrogenetic environments that favour extreme enrichment of incompatible elements. Carbonatite deposits dominate world resources because they derive from mantle melts with high volatile content, strong fractionation potential, and prolonged intrusive histories. Bayan Obo, Mountain Pass, and Mount Weld remain the key examples. Their mineralogical profiles include bastnäsite, monazite, synchysite, and fluorcarbonates with accessory barite, fluorite, magnetite, and apatite.

These deposits exhibit broad ore zones with varying grade, alteration intensity, and rare earth distribution controlled by magmatic differentiation and hydrothermal re mobilisation. Their massive tonnage and predictable mineralogy enable long term industrial planning.

In contrast, ion adsorption clay deposits represent a unique style of rare earth enrichment linked to tropical weathering of felsic igneous rocks. Southern China hosts the majority of these deposits due to climate, topography, and granitic parent lithology. Granites contain allanite, apatite, monazite, zircon, and xenotime as primary rare earth bearing minerals. Prolonged leaching releases trivalent ions that bind to clay surfaces through outer sphere complexation. Heavy rare earths show strong selective retention, which produces a profile dominated by yttrium, dysprosium, terbium, holmium, and erbium. Grades remain low but extraction cost stays low due to simple leaching. These deposits underpin the heavy rare earth supply chain and influence global market structure.

Australia has emerged as a major supplier due to high grade carbonatite and alkaline deposits. Mount Weld remains the most advanced. Nolans Bore provides a large fluoroapatite monazite xenotime system enriched in neodymium and praseodymium with trace heavy rare earths. The Dubbo project targets a zirconia rare earth niobium hafnium system within alkaline intrusive rocks. These systems offer diversified rare earth output and complement light rare earth dominant deposits in other continents. Australia's stable regulatory environment and robust infrastructure support long term investment in these projects.

Greenland's peralkaline intrusive complexes provide some of the world's largest undeveloped rare earth resources. The Kvanefjeld project within the Ilimaussaq complex contains eudialyte with significant light and heavy rare earth content along with uranium and zinc. The Kringlerne deposit contains similar mineralogy with high tonnage potential. These deposits face processing hurdles due to eudialyte reactivity and silica management, yet they offer strategic diversification for countries seeking alternative supply outside East Asia. Cold climate logistics, environmental assessment requirements, and uranium associated permitting influence project timelines.

Canada hosts numerous advanced rare earth prospects. The Nechalacho deposit in the Northwest Territories contains bastnäsite, monazite, xenotime, and fergusonite within layered alkaline intrusions. Its upper zone contains light rare earths, while the deeper zone contains heavy rare earths. Strange Lake on the Quebec Labrador border contains eudialyte rich peralkaline granites with high heavy rare earth content. These deposits provide strategic potential for North American supply chains, yet they remain constrained by remote location, harsh climate, and complex mineralogy requiring specialised processing.

Africa includes both placer and hard rock deposits. Steenkampskraal in South Africa contains high grade monazite veins with significant thorium and uranium. This deposit offers high neodymium and praseodymium content with manageable heavy rare earth fractions. Ngualla in Tanzania provides a weathered carbonatite with bastnäsite rich ore in its upper zones. The deposit shows favourable mineralogy and moderate heavy rare earth content. Madagascar's Toliara and Ambatovy regions host coastal mineral sands with monazite and xenotime. These sands integrate with existing ilmenite and zircon operations, offering co product rare earth potential.

Russia and Central Asia contain large alkaline and carbonatite systems with rare earth potential. The Tomtor deposit in Siberia contains rare earth rich peralkaline rocks with high niobium and heavy rare earth concentrations. Kyrgyzstan and Kazakhstan host carbonatite complexes and placer systems under evaluation. These regions hold long term supply potential but remain influenced by infrastructure gaps, regulatory complexity, and geopolitical considerations.

This distribution highlights the concentration of globally significant deposits within specific geological contexts. The interplay between mineralogy, climate, infrastructure, and regulatory frameworks determines which deposits reach production and how they shape global supply.

Major global rare earth deposits fit into a small number of high productivity geological categories, and each category shapes the global supply chain by controlling access to specific rare earth profiles. Carbonatite systems deliver high volumes of light rare earths. Ion adsorption clays deliver heavy rare earths. Peralkaline intrusive complexes deliver mixed profiles with long term scalability. Heavy mineral sands deliver stable monazite and xenotime concentrates that complement hard rock production. These deposit classes underpin all global production models.

Carbonatite megasystems such as Bayan Obo and Mountain Pass anchor the light rare earth supply due to exceptional tonnage and favourable mineralogy. Bayan Obo's extraordinary size arises from repeated magmatic intrusions, metasomatism, and structural deformation that redistributed rare earths across multiple stratigraphic units. Its ore zones display grades far above global norms because mineralising events concentrated bastnäsite and monazite into replacement bodies and breccia zones. Mountain Pass benefits from simple mineralogy dominated by bastnäsite with minimal thorium content, which reduces radiological complexity. Mount Weld's weathering profile increases extraction efficiency by liberating secondary phosphates and oxides. These deposits allow cost efficient beneficiation and large scale solvent extraction, making them central to global supply forecasts.

Ion adsorption clays represent the most important heavy rare earth source due to selective retention of elements such as dysprosium, terbium, holmium, and erbium. Their genesis depends on subtropical climate, granitic parent lithology, and long term leaching. China controls most known deposits, giving it strategic leverage in magnet and defence related industries. New exploration confirmed similar weathering environments in Myanmar, Madagascar, Vietnam, and Laos, yet geological, environmental, and social factors limit consistent supply. Ion adsorption clay deposits remain low grade but offer unique processing advantages, including ambient temperature leaching, minimal comminution, and lower chemical intensity. They continue to shape the heavy rare earth market despite limited tonnage.

Peralkaline intrusive complexes offer long term expansion potential because they host large rare earth inventories with mixed light and heavy rare earth content. Greenland's Ilimaussaq complex contains multi billion tonne eudialyte bodies with both light and heavy rare earth enrichment. Strange Lake in Canada, Kipawa in Quebec, and Norra Kärr in Sweden contain similar mineralogical profiles. Processing these deposits remains challenging due to silica gel formation during leaching, the need for tailored reagents, and complex mineralogy with multiple substituting ions. Their strategic value lies in scale, jurisdictional stability, and the potential to diversify away from dominant producers once metallurgical routes mature.

Heavy mineral sands provide co product rare earth feedstock through monazite and xenotime concentrates. Operations in Madagascar, Mozambique, Kenya, South Africa, and Australia produce heavy mineral sands for titanium and zircon industries. Monazite and xenotime represent a valuable secondary stream with high rare earth content. Their processing requires radiological controls, yet these concentrates provide a stable supplementary source with well established beneficiation methods. New projects aim to integrate monazite recovery into existing mineral sands operations to enhance supply without building new mines.

South America holds several carbonatite and alkaline prospects with long term potential. Brazil's Araxá and Catalão complexes contain rare earth enriched apatite and monazite associated with phosphate operations. These systems remain under evaluation due to regulatory factors and infrastructure requirements. Argentina and Bolivia contain alkaline complexes with rare earth mineralisation linked to tectonic and magmatic provinces associated with continental rifting.

India and Sri Lanka contain extensive placer deposits with monazite rich heavy mineral sands. Historical operations extracted monazite for thorium production, leaving sizeable tailings with rare earth potential. Modern development faces radiological regulation and environmental review, yet these regions hold some of the highest monazite concentrations worldwide.

This global distribution shows that rare earth resources remain abundant yet constrained by mineralogy, jurisdiction, climate, and processing requirements. Major deposits define supply patterns through their scale, composition, and metallurgical complexity. Their evolution over time dictates global production, strategic planning, and market behaviour.

2.3 Extraction potential in under-developed regions

Extraction potential in under developed regions depends on geological endowment, mineralogical complexity, infrastructure capability, regulatory conditions, and access to hydrometallurgical technology. Many of these regions hold large rare earth inventories across carbonatite complexes, alkaline intrusions, ion adsorption clay analogues, and heavy mineral sands. Their development lags due to processing constraints rather than geological scarcity. Comprehensive evaluation requires assessment of ore type, grade distribution, weathering profile, clay mineralogy, and proximity to transport, water, and power.

Africa holds some of the most promising under developed systems. Tanzania's Ngualla deposit contains a deeply weathered carbonatite with highly liberated bastnäsite in the upper horizon. Weathering removes carbonate gangue and concentrates rare earths into a clay rich matrix that improves acid leach kinetics. This reduces comminution demands and supports lower OPEX than many hard rock systems. Additional carbonatite occurrences across Malawi, Kenya, Namibia, and Angola display similar potential. Their extraction depends on establishing regional processing hubs that share solvent extraction infrastructure. Small scale dispersed operations remain unviable due to the large number of mixer settler stages required for full separation. The lack of refining capacity prevents these deposits from entering the global supply chain at scale.

Madagascar, Mozambique, and Tanzania host heavy mineral sands with monazite and xenotime that offer reliable extraction potential. These sands contain high density, mechanically robust grains that respond well to gravity, magnetic, and electrostatic separation. Plants already operate for ilmenite and zircon, which allows monazite recovery as a co product. Radiological regulations remain the primary barrier because monazite contains thorium and uranium. Establishing controlled waste management systems and long term monitoring facilities is essential for unlocking extraction potential. These deposits provide steady volumes that could support regional rare earth concentrate production if regulatory frameworks align with international standards.

Across Southeast Asia, several under explored granitic belts show conditions favourable for ion adsorption clay formation. Myanmar, Laos, Thailand, and Vietnam contain vast regions of tropical weathering with high rainfall and felsic parent rock composition. Systematic exploration confirms the presence of clay hosted rare earths with heavy rare earth dominance similar to Chinese clays. Extraction potential depends on controlled leaching systems that avoid ammonium discharge and soil degradation. Environmental oversight remains limited in some jurisdictions, which restricts commercial investment. Developing sustainable leaching circuits with closed loop ammonium recovery and modular adsorption units could unlock significant heavy rare earth supply.

South America holds multiple alkaline and carbonatite complexes with under evaluated rare earth potential. Brazil's Araxá, Catalão, and Juquiá systems contain monazite and apatite enriched zones with favourable rare earth profiles. Bolivia, Argentina, and Colombia host peralkaline systems with eudialyte and zirconium rich mineral assemblages. Infrastructure gaps, limited metallurgy expertise, and regulatory complexity slow development. Many deposits remain at early drill stage because capital markets prioritise gold, copper, and lithium over rare earths. These regions could supply diversified feedstocks to global markets once processing hubs emerge.

Central Asia contains carbonatite and alkaline systems across Kazakhstan, Kyrgyzstan, and Mongolia. These deposits sit in remote high altitude regions with limited infrastructure. Their mineralogy includes bastnäsite, monazite, and niobium rich minerals that allow co product strategies. Extraction remains constrained by transport networks, water availability, and energy cost. Hydrometallurgical circuits require stable power and controlled reagent supply, both of which remain challenging in remote areas. Building integrated processing zones with rail access and shared infrastructure would expand extraction potential.

The Middle East holds smaller rare earth occurrences within alkaline granites and carbonatites, especially in Saudi Arabia and Jordan. These systems remain under drilled and under sampled. Their extraction potential depends on detailed mineralogical characterisation, as many prospects contain low grade diffuse mineralisation rather than discrete ore bodies. Regional investment in downstream processing could change economic viability because proximity to ports and industrial zones reduces logistics cost.

Under developed regions hold substantial geological resources, yet require coordinated development of beneficiation, leaching, and separation facilities. Extraction potential hinges on refining capacity rather than ore availability. Once separation hubs expand, these regions will become important suppliers in the global rare earth industry.

Extraction potential in under developed regions hinges on mineralogical readiness and the feasibility of integrating advanced processing routes into environments with limited industrial infrastructure. Rare earth ore requires precise beneficiation, controlled roasting, selective leaching, and extensive solvent extraction. These stages demand reliable water, electricity, transport corridors, chemical supply chains, and qualified personnel. Many under developed regions hold high quality geological resources yet lack these supporting systems. Investment strategies must therefore examine the alignment between local geology and regional industrial capability.

African hard rock deposits present strong extraction potential because weathering enhances mineral liberation and improves leachability. Ngualla in Tanzania, Songwe Hill in Malawi, Kangankunde in Malawi, and Lofdal in Namibia contain bastnäsite, monazite, and xenotime within weathered carbonatites. Thick saprolite profiles reduce grinding energy requirement and expose minerals to acid digestion more effectively than fresh rock. Rare earths partition into secondary phosphate phases that show improved reactivity. These characteristics lower operational cost. Processing constraints remain tied to the absence of solvent extraction plants. Establishing regional separation hubs could deliver economies of scale and reduce the burden on individual projects. Such hubs would process mixed rare earth concentrates from multiple mines, enabling shared infrastructure for leaching, precipitation, solvent extraction, and waste management.

Ion adsorption clay analogues in Southeast Asia offer heavy rare earth potential. Myanmar holds extensive clay deposits with heavy rare earth enrichment. Myanmar's geology mirrors that of southern China, with deeply weathered granitic terrains and high rainfall. Extraction uses ammonium sulphate or magnesium salts to desorb rare earth ions from clay surfaces. Current operations remain small scale and produce variable grades due to inconsistent leaching practices. Industrial scale potential requires adoption of column leaching, controlled solution circulation, ammonium recovery systems, and environmental monitoring. Vietnam hosts similar clay systems in its central highlands. Laos and Thailand show prospective granitic belts but lack systematic sampling, mineralogical studies, and adsorption modelling. With proper environmental controls, these regions hold capacity to become major suppliers of heavy rare earths.

South America holds significant but under evaluated deposits. Brazil's mineral provinces contain numerous alkaline intrusions and carbonatite complexes with rare earth enrichment. These include Catalão, Araxá, Barra do Itapirapuã, and Poços de Caldas. Rare earth minerals appear within apatite, monazite, and pyroclore assemblages derived from magmatic and hydrothermal processes. Extraction potential depends on integration with existing phosphate and niobium operations. Co production strategies reduce capital cost by sharing mining, crushing, and beneficiation infrastructure. Processing challenges include thorium content, complex mineralogy, and high acid consumption. Argentina and Bolivia contain peralkaline systems with eudialyte and zirconium rich mineralisation. These rocks require advanced leaching technologies due to silica gel formation. Regional adoption of chloride based leaching circuits could unlock these systems.

Central Asian deposits display large tonnage potential but remain unexploited due to infrastructure gaps. Tomtor in Siberia contains some of the highest heavy rare earth and niobium grades globally. Its mineralogy includes eudialyte, loparite, and pyrochlore within peralkaline rocks. Extraction depends on establishing processing plants capable of handling complex feedstock with high impurity load. Kazakhstan and Kyrgyzstan hold carbonatite complexes with bastnäsite and monazite that mirror early stage deposits in Africa. Their development depends on power availability, transport links to industrial hubs, and stable regulatory frameworks. These regions remain promising but require long term investment planning.

Middle Eastern alkaline granites and carbonatite occurrences in Saudi Arabia, Jordan, and Egypt contain trace to moderate rare earth enrichment. Detailed mineralogical analysis is needed to identify workable ore bodies. Some of these systems contain monazite rich zones that respond to sulphuric acid digestion. Their extraction potential depends on linking mining operations with industrial zones that supply chemicals, reagents, and energy. These countries hold strategic interest in diversifying industrial capability and may invest directly in refining capacity.

Extraction potential in under developed regions reflects alignment between geology and processing capability. These regions hold significant rare earth resources. Their development requires coordinated investment in beneficiation, hydrometallurgy, and solvent extraction infrastructure. Once separation capacity expands geographically, many under developed regions will become major contributors to global supply.

Extraction potential in under developed regions depends on converting geological resources into operational supply chains capable of producing separated rare earth oxides. This conversion requires staged capacity building. Each stage introduces distinct technical and economic barriers. Early evaluation involves mineralogical mapping, lithogeochemical sampling, hyperspectral imaging, and geostatistical modelling. Many under developed regions lack consistent exploration frameworks, resulting in under sampled carbonatite rings, uncharacterised alkaline complexes, and poorly defined clay profiles. Improving early stage sampling and applying portable X ray fluorescence, laser induced breakdown spectroscopy, and mineral liberation analysis would drastically increase resource confidence across these terrains.

Beneficiation presents the next barrier. Hard rock deposits in Africa, Central Asia, and South America contain intergrown rare earth minerals with variable grain size. Achieving efficient liberation requires fine grinding with strict control of particle size distribution. Under developed regions often lack access to high energy mills, hydrocyclone clusters, and advanced flotation cells. Without controlled flotation chemistry and frother dosage, recovery remains inconsistent. Establishing regional beneficiation centres with shared comminution and flotation equipment would reduce capital intensity for individual projects. These centres could process ore from multiple mines, producing standardised rare earth mineral concentrates suitable for leaching.

Processing heavy mineral sands offers more immediate extraction potential because beneficiation relies on well established physical separation methods. Many coastal regions in Africa, India, and Southeast Asia already operate titanium and zircon plants. Integrating monazite and xenotime recovery into these circuits requires additional magnetic and electrostatic separation steps. The primary barrier is regulatory, not technical. Radiological controls for thorium rich monazite require encapsulation, transport protocols, and long term storage solutions. Establishing regional radiological management frameworks based on international standards would unlock significant monazite volumes currently rejected as waste.

Ion adsorption clays in Myanmar, Vietnam, Laos, and Madagascar offer the simplest extraction route but require strict environmental safeguards. Small scale leaching operations produce inconsistent grades due to uncontrolled ammonium application and lack of solution recycling. Scaling extraction requires transition to column leaching, solution recirculation, ammonium recovery, and pH controlled desorption. These technologies demand trained personnel and consistent reagent supply. Creating modular leaching units deployable across multiple clay basins would stabilise output and reduce environmental impact. With proper oversight, these regions could challenge China's dominance in heavy rare earth production.

Hydrometallurgical capacity remains the critical bottleneck. Solvent extraction plants require thousands of mixer settler stages for full separation. The concentration of this technology in a few countries restricts global supply. Under developed regions rarely possess the chemical engineering expertise, organic solvent production, and waste treatment capacity required to operate large solvent extraction circuits. Establishing regional hubs with state supported investment, international partnerships, and technology transfer agreements would transform extraction potential. These hubs could process imported concentrates from neighbouring countries, creating integrated rare earth corridors similar to existing copper and aluminium clusters.

Infrastructure remains a decisive factor. Rare earth mining requires reliable power, consistent water supply, and road or rail networks capable of transporting bulk concentrate to processing facilities. Many geologically rich regions in Africa and Central Asia sit far from industrial centres. Building dedicated corridors with power generation, water pipelines, and rail access would unlock large volumes of rare earth resources currently stranded by logistics. Such infrastructure could support co production of niobium, phosphates, fluorite, and zircon, improving project economics.

Institutional frameworks also influence extraction potential. Stable mining codes, predictable royalty regimes, transparent permitting, and environmental oversight allow long term planning. Many under developed regions hold attractive geology but lack regulatory predictability. Reforming these frameworks would reduce investment risk and expand exploration, particularly for deep or complex deposits that require sustained drilling.

Under developed regions hold rare earth inventories large enough to reshape global supply once beneficiation hubs, hydrometallurgical plants, environmental safeguards, and logistics corridors mature. These regions represent the next major source of supply growth as existing producers reach maturity and global demand for electric motors, wind turbines, and advanced electronics accelerates.

2.4 Factors influencing deposit quality

Deposit quality depends on a combination of geological, mineralogical, geochemical, and structural parameters that determine grade, tonnage, and processing performance. Rare earth deposits vary widely because rare earth enrichment requires specific magmatic, hydrothermal, or weathering processes capable of concentrating incompatible elements beyond crustal background levels. Geological setting provides the first control. Carbonatite systems deliver high grades when fractional crystallisation, melt immiscibility, and volatile driven transport align to produce concentrated bastnäsite or monazite zones. Peralkaline complexes require extended differentiation to allow rare earths to partition into late stage silicate, zirconium, and titanate phases. Ion adsorption clays need prolonged subtropical weathering to release rare earths from primary minerals and bind them to clay surfaces. Each environment imposes its own quality constraints and dictates the range of elements enriched.

Mineralogy remains the strongest determinant of deposit quality because it dictates extraction route, processing cost, and achievable recoveries. Bastnäsite offers favourable liberation and leaching behaviour under controlled roasting or direct acid digestion. Monazite confers high grade but contains thorium and uranium, which increase regulatory burden and waste management cost. Xenotime hosts heavy rare earths but displays high lattice energy and chemical resistance, which reduces leach efficiency. Allanite produces fine grained weathering products that complicate beneficiation. Eudialyte holds both light and heavy rare earths but releases silica gels during leaching, which interfere with hydrometallurgical circuits. Mineralogical composition therefore determines whether a deposit supports low cost leaching or requires complex roasting, phase decomposition, or chloride based circuits. Deposits with simple bastnäsite dominant mineralogy offer higher quality due to predictable extraction behaviour. Grade distribution influences deposit quality through its impact on mining rate, cut off grade, and revenue per tonne. Rare earth grades vary widely across systems, from below one tenth of a percent in ion adsorption clays to more than ten percent in weathered carbonatites. High grades reduce mining and processing cost per unit of rare earth oxide because less gangue material requires comminution and leaching. Uniform grade distribution improves mine planning by reducing dilution. Strong vertical zoning in weathered profiles or complex lateral grade variations reduce operational stability. Deposits with consistent high grade zones and predictable changes across depth deliver better quality and longer mine life under stable cost conditions.

Host rock chemistry controls metallurgical performance. Carbonatite systems offer desirable host rocks because carbonate gangue responds well to roasting and acid digestion. Silicate rich host rocks complicate leaching due to silica polymerisation and high acid consumption. Fluorine rich rocks create volatile fluorine species during roasting that require specialised off gas treatment. Phosphate rich host rocks improve rare earth retention but require aggressive digestion. Deposits with favourable host rock chemistry minimise reagent use, reduce waste volumes, and improve overall processing efficiency.

Weathering profile thickness shapes the extractive potential of carbonatite and granitic systems. Deep weathering enhances liberation of rare earth minerals and reduces the degree of comminution required. Weathered profiles convert resistant phases into secondary minerals more amenable to extraction. In clay hosted systems, weathering profile controls adsorption capacity, heavy rare earth fraction, and depth of enrichment. Thick, well developed saprolite with strong leaching horizons increases deposit quality because rare earth ions accumulate at defined depths where clay minerals remain stable. Weakly developed profiles produce diffuse concentrations that lack economic viability.

Structural controls influence ore continuity and grade concentration. Faults, fractures, and shear zones act as pathways for rare earth bearing fluids and create veins, breccia zones, and replacement bodies with higher grade than surrounding rock. Structural dilation zones host large ore bodies because they accommodate volumes of mineralising fluids.

Conversely, complex faulting can disrupt ore zones and reduce continuity, increasing exploration and drilling cost. Deposits within stable structural domains with predictable geometry offer higher quality and more efficient mine scheduling.

Deposit quality reflects the interaction of mineralogical, structural, geochemical, and weathering processes. These factors govern grade, extraction difficulty, environmental burden, and long term economic performance.

Deposit quality depends strongly on textural characteristics that control liberation, beneficiation efficiency, and leaching behaviour. Grain size distribution influences how rare earth minerals respond to crushing and grinding. Coarse bastnäsite or monazite crystals liberate at moderate grind sizes, reducing energy consumption and improving flotation performance. Fine grained intergrowths require intense grinding to achieve adequate liberation, which increases operating cost and produces slimes that interfere with flotation and magnetic separation. Eudialyte rich deposits often show microcrystalline textures that trap rare earths within complex silicate matrices, reducing liberation even at very fine particle sizes. Allanite rich deposits suffer from heterogeneous textures that produce wide liberation curves. Deposits with homogeneous coarse grained mineralisation offer higher quality due to lower comminution cost and more efficient downstream processing.

Mineral associations also influence quality. Carbonatite hosted deposits with bastnäsite or monazite associated with fluorite, barite, and calcite provide favourable beneficiation conditions because these gangue minerals respond predictably to flotation. In contrast, deposits where rare earth minerals occur with iron oxides, amphiboles, or mica require more complex reagent regimes. Iron rich gangue reduces selectivity in flotation and increases acid consumption in leaching circuits. Mica rich ores create viscous slurries that challenge thickening and filtering. Silicate gangue produces silica gel during digestion, which clogs equipment and reduces leach efficiency. Deposits with favourable gangue associations minimise complications in beneficiation and hydrometallurgy.

Geochemical zonation shapes deposit quality by determining the distribution of light and heavy rare earths. Light rare earth rich zones suit applications in catalysts, polishing powders, and magnet feedstocks. Heavy rare earth rich zones provide dysprosium, terbium, holmium, and erbium needed for high temperature magnets and advanced optical systems. Deposits with balanced distribution of light and heavy elements hold greater commercial flexibility because they meet multiple market segments. Ion adsorption clays hold strategic value due to their heavy rare earth enrichment. Carbonatites provide high tonnage light rare earths but require complementary feedstocks to supply heavy elements. Deposits dominated by a single segment face larger price volatility risk.

Impurity levels influence deposit quality because impurities raise processing cost and complicate regulatory frameworks. Thorium and uranium occur as lattice bound impurities in monazite and xenotime. These impurities require controlled waste storage, environmental permits, and radiological monitoring. High thorium content reduces economic viability unless co product strategies or thorium markets emerge. Iron rich deposits require additional steps to manage iron hydroxide precipitates. Fluorine in bastnäsite requires specialised off gas treatment during roasting. Phosphorus in monazite modifies leach chemistry and increases scaling risk in reactors. Deposits with low impurity load support simpler extraction routes and reduce environmental liability.

Hydrothermal overprinting influences deposit quality by modifying mineralogy, texture, and grade. Hydrothermal fluids re distribute rare earths, convert primary minerals into secondary phases, and produce veins with upgraded grade. In some deposits, hydrothermal alteration improves quality by increasing rare earth concentration and producing minerals more amenable to leaching. In others, alteration introduces fine grained phosphates or carbonate veinlets that reduce metallurgical performance. Quality improves when alteration enhances liberation and leachable mineralogy. It declines when alteration increases mineralogical complexity or introduces refractory phases.

Deposit size and continuity also influence quality. Large, continuous ore bodies support bulk mining methods, stable throughput, and predictable cash flow. Small, fragmented lenses create operational variability, increase dilution, and require selective mining. Continuity depends on magmatic emplacement patterns, structural stability, and weathering processes. Deposits with well defined geometry, thick ore zones, and limited structural disruption deliver higher quality and lower operational risk.

Environmental context influences extraction feasibility. Deposits in arid regions require water import, desalination, or water recycling systems. Deposits in remote high altitude areas require costly transport corridors. Deposits in tropical regions may face intense rainfall that complicates tailings management. Quality improves when environmental conditions support stable operations with manageable risk.

Deposit quality emerges from a mosaic of geological and operational factors. Successful rare earth projects align favourable mineralogy, manageable impurities, coherent geometry, and accessible infrastructure.

Deposit quality depends on how mineralogical, geochemical, and environmental factors interact with extraction technology, cost structures, and long term project risk. Rare earth mining demands integrated performance across exploration, beneficiation, leaching, separation, waste management, and logistics. A deposit with strong intrinsic geology can still deliver poor economic quality if it misaligns with technological capacity or external conditions.

Process compatibility forms one of the strongest quality drivers. Deposits that align naturally with established flowsheets offer higher value because they avoid long development cycles. Bastnäsite dominant deposits suit flotation, calcination, and hydrochloric or sulphuric acid digestion. Ion adsorption clays align with ambient temperature salt leaching. Monazite rich sands integrate with existing heavy mineral circuits. Deposits requiring new technology, such as eudialyte rich bodies needing chloride leaching with silica suppression, remain high risk until pilot scale validation confirms stable performance. Process risk reduces deposit quality because investors discount operations that depend on unproven chemistry or complex plant configurations.

Energy intensity influences deposit quality by dictating operating cost. Rare earth extraction requires energy for comminution, roasting, solvent extraction pumps, and thermal treatment of waste. Carbonatite hosted deposits with weathered profiles require less comminution. Ion adsorption clays require minimal energy for leaching. Fresh hard rock in peralkaline complexes requires high energy input because microcrystalline silicates resist grinding. Deposits located near low cost energy sources, such as hydroelectric grids or gas powered industrial zones, offer structural cost advantages. Those in remote areas with diesel dependence face higher cost profiles and reduced quality.

Water availability also shapes quality. Leaching, flotation, and solvent extraction require consistent water supply with controlled chemistry. High sulphate, chloride, or carbonate levels in local water sources alter reagent performance. Deposits in arid regions require desalination or deep groundwater extraction, which increases cost. Clay hosted deposits in tropical regions sometimes suffer from excessive rainfall, producing dilute leach solutions and complicating recovery. High quality deposits align with water conditions that support stable process chemistry without major treatment infrastructure.

Infrastructure proximity influences quality because rare earth supply chains require transport of bulk ore, concentrate, reagents, and waste. Deposits near ports, rail, and industrial zones offer lower logistics cost. Remote deposits require new roads, power lines, or airstrips. The cost of building this infrastructure often exceeds initial mining cost. High altitude deposits face cold weather constraints that slow construction and increase energy demand. Deposits near existing mining clusters benefit from shared infrastructure and established service industries, enhancing quality.

Environmental and regulatory context defines long term viability. Rare earth extraction produces waste streams with radionuclides, fluorine species, and acid residues. Deposits with manageable impurity levels reduce environmental liability. Monazite rich deposits with high thorium content require multi decade monitoring of tailings. Carbonatite deposits with low radionuclide content offer better environmental profiles. Jurisdictions with predictable permitting frameworks improve project quality because investors trust approval timelines. Regions with unstable regulation, overlapping land claims, or inconsistent environmental enforcement reduce perceived quality regardless of geological potential.

Social and geopolitical factors also influence deposit quality. Deposits in politically stable regions with strong legal systems receive higher valuation. Projects in conflict zones or regions with weak governance face security risk and supply disruption. Community relations influence access, land use, and long term operation. Deposits with minimal displacement impact or strong community support offer higher quality because they reduce social risk. National strategic policies influence project trajectory. Governments may prioritise domestic processing, impose export restrictions, or mandate value addition. These policies alter project economics and influence quality assessments.

Market alignment further shapes quality. Deposits rich in neodymium and praseodymium hold higher quality due to magnet demand. Deposits with high dysprosium or terbium content hold strategic value due to limited global supply. Deposits dominated by cerium or lanthanum hold lower value due to oversupply. Quality improves when the deposit's rare earth distribution matches long term industrial demand.

Deposit quality reflects how geology, mineralogy, metallurgy, infrastructure, regulation, and market forces interact. Rare earth deposits with favourable mineralogy, stable grade, low impurity content, strong infrastructure support, and high strategic relevance deliver superior long term value within the global supply chain.

3. Mining and Processing Technologies
3.1 Exploration methods and ore evaluation

Exploration for rare earth deposits requires integrated geological, geophysical, and geochemical techniques that identify zones where incompatible elements accumulated during magmatic differentiation, hydrothermal activity, or deep weathering. Each exploration method targets specific signatures linked to mineralogy, host rock chemistry, or alteration patterns. Effective programmes combine remote sensing, field mapping, structural analysis, and subsurface sampling to establish grade continuity, mineral associations, and extraction potential.

Geological mapping forms the foundation of exploration. Field teams identify lithological boundaries, intrusive relationships, alteration halos, breccia zones, carbonatite dykes, alkaline intrusions, and pegmatitic bodies. Mapping focuses on locating fluorine rich veining, carbonate replacement textures, fenite alteration, and structural conduits that indicate rare earth mobilisation. Detailed petrography confirms the presence of bastnäsite, monazite, xenotime, allanite, or eudialyte. Mineralogical logging identifies grain size, texture, intergrowths, and alteration intensity. These features control future beneficiation performance and directly influence ore quality. Early mineralogical assessment determines whether a deposit will require simple flotation and leaching or complex roasting and chloride digestion.

Geophysical methods enhance targeting by detecting density, magnetic, radiometric, and electrical contrasts linked to rare earth mineralisation. Magnetic surveys identify carbonatite and alkaline intrusive bodies due to associated magnetite enrichment. High resolution aeromagnetic grids reveal ring structures, dykes, and intrusive centres. Radiometric surveys detect thorium and potassium anomalies associated with monazite, xenotime, and altered granites. This method provides effective screening for placer and hard rock monazite systems. Gravity surveys define dense carbonatite cores, breccia pipes, and feeder zones. Electromagnetic and induced polarisation surveys identify clay rich weathering profiles and hydrothermally altered zones. Integrated geophysical interpretation allows delineation of drill targets, especially where surface exposure remains limited.

Geochemical exploration uses soil, stream sediment, and rock sampling to identify rare earth anomalies. Soil geochemistry identifies ion adsorption clay systems when heavy rare earth enrichment correlates with clay dominated horizons. Stream sediment surveys detect resistant minerals such as monazite and xenotime that concentrate in alluvial environments. Rock chip sampling in carbonatite and alkaline complexes reveals light and heavy rare earth patterns through chondrite normalised signatures. These signatures help classify mineralising processes and guide drilling. Multi element diagrams reveal accompanying geochemical markers such as Nb, Sr, Ba, P, and F that confirm magmatic affinity. Element ratio analysis, including La Nd, Dy Tb, and Y Ho, refines understanding of fractionation and primary source processes.

Drilling provides the definitive dataset for ore evaluation. Core drilling allows continuous sampling, structural analysis, and mineralogical characterisation. Core logging captures lithology, alteration, vein density, breccia textures, weathering profile thickness, and mineral distribution. Assay intervals reveal grade variability, heavy to light rare earth ratios, and vertical zonation. Density measurements determine tonnage estimates. Core samples undergo mineralogical and metallurgical testing, including quantitative evaluation of minerals by scanning electron microscopy, laser ablation, and electron microprobe analysis. These tests identify liberation size, mineral associations, and impurity levels such as thorium and uranium. Drill spacing must balance cost and statistical confidence. Tight spacing increases resource classification accuracy for measured and indicated categories.

Bulk sampling supports metallurgical evaluation. Large volumes of representative material are required to simulate industrial grinding, flotation, roasting, and leaching. Pilot scale tests determine recovery, reagent consumption, gangue behaviour, and waste generation. These results provide the basis for economic evaluation and flowsheet selection. Deposits with favourable metallurgy progress to pre feasibility studies. Those with complex mineralogy may require additional bench scale optimisation before advancing.

Ore evaluation integrates geological, geophysical, geochemical, and metallurgical data into three dimensional resource models. Geostatistical methods interpolate grade across the deposit using variograms tailored to rare earth distribution. Modelling considers lithological domains, structural boundaries, and weathering zones. Engineers calculate tonnage, grade, heavy to light rare earth distribution, strip ratio, and waste volume. Ore evaluation also considers energy intensity, water demand, reagent consumption, and impurity load. These factors define whether the deposit supports commercial development.

Exploration requires integration of advanced remote sensing and mineralogical tools that identify key spectral, structural, and geochemical markers linked to rare earth enrichment. Remote sensing supports early stage reconnaissance across large terrains. Hyperspectral imaging detects spectral features associated with carbonate, phosphate, clay, and iron oxide alteration. Carbonatite related systems show diagnostic absorption bands linked to calcite, dolomite, and fluorite. Peralkaline complexes show spectral signatures from nepheline, alkali feldspar, and associated alteration minerals. Weathered granitic terrains with ion adsorption potential show clay dominated spectra with kaolinite, halloysite, and gibbsite features. Satellite based multispectral data complements hyperspectral imagery by revealing structural corridors, ring complexes, dykes, and hydrothermal footprints. Airborne gamma spectrometry identifies thorium and potassium anomalies that correlate with monazite and granitic sources.

Mineralogical tools refine exploration targeting. Automated mineralogy systems use scanning electron microscopy to classify mineral phases, grain size, and liberation characteristics. These systems quantify bastnäsite, monazite, xenotime, allanite, eudialyte, and associated gangue. Mineral liberation analysis links texture with likely processing routes. Electron microprobe analysis determines elemental distributions and substitution mechanisms within mineral lattices. Understanding lattice occupancy helps predict impurity content and geochemical zoning. Raman spectroscopy and infrared spectroscopy identify carbonate, silicate, and phosphate phases rapidly in the field or laboratory. Portable X ray fluorescence supports rapid identification of rare earth pathfinder elements such as hafnium, niobium, zirconium, and thorium.

Drilling strategies depend on deposit style. Carbonatite and alkaline systems require oriented core drilling to capture intrusive geometry, dyke orientation, and breccia distribution. Drill holes target ring structures, feeder zones, and magnetite rich units. Hole spacing tightens within high grade domains to establish continuity and define economic boundaries. Ion adsorption clay systems require shallow drilling with careful horizon sampling. Drilling must capture vertical zoning in clay profiles, including upper leached zones, middle adsorption zones, and lower saprolite transition. Bulk density measurements must account for moisture content and swelling behaviour in clay rich horizons.

Sampling protocols require strict quality control. Representative sampling prevents grade overestimation or underestimation. Core splitting, duplicate sampling, blank insertion, and certified reference materials ensure analytical accuracy. Chain of custody and laboratory auditing reduce sampling bias. Assays typically measure individual rare earth oxides and impurity elements. Interpretation requires normalisation to chondrite values to reveal fractionation patterns and identify light or heavy rare earth enrichment.

Ore evaluation requires integration of mineralogical, metallurgical, and economic data. Bench scale tests assess comminution behaviour through Bond work index tests and particle size distribution analysis. Flotation tests determine reagent sensitivity, surface activation behaviour, and selectivity between rare earth minerals and gangue. Roasting tests evaluate thermal decomposition of fluorocarbonates, phosphates, and silicates. Acid and alkali leaching tests determine dissolution rates, impurity solubility, and reagent consumption. Solvent extraction tests evaluate distribution coefficients, separation factors, and organic phase stability.

Pilot scale tests validate bench scale findings and identify operational constraints. Continuous pilot operations simulate grinding, flotation, roasting, leaching, solid liquid separation, solvent extraction, and oxalate precipitation. These tests identify scaling risks, organic losses, residue characteristics, and water balance requirements. Data from pilot operations feed into mass balance models, flow diagrams, and engineering design.

Resource classification follows JORC, NI 43 101, or CRIRSCO standards. These frameworks require clear demonstration of geological continuity, sampling reliability, and reasonable prospects for eventual economic extraction. Deposits with well constrained geometry, tight drill spacing, and favourable metallurgy achieve measured or indicated classifications. Those with limited drilling or uncertain metallurgy remain inferred. Resource classification influences investor confidence and determines whether a project advances toward feasibility.

Ore evaluation integrates technical and economic considerations. Projects with favourable mineralogy, strong grade, stable metallurgy, and supportive infrastructure progress toward development. Those with refractory mineralogy, complex impurity profiles, or high processing cost remain speculative.

Ore evaluation extends beyond geological and metallurgical criteria. It requires quantitative assessment of technical risk, operational resilience, and long term extraction performance. Rare earth deposits present distinct challenges because each element contributes different value and requires its own separation pathway. Ore evaluation therefore analyses not only grade but the distribution of individual rare earths, impurity load, and the compatibility of the ore with downstream separation infrastructure.

Advanced geostatistics plays a central role in evaluating ore distribution. Three dimensional block models interpolate grade, density, mineralogical domains, and weathering profiles. Variogram analysis reveals spatial continuity and directional anisotropy. Carbonatite deposits often show strong vertical continuity due to magmatic emplacement, while ion adsorption clays show stratified continuity linked to weathering processes. Peralkaline deposits may show irregular zoning due to complex magmatic history. Multiple indicator kriging or co kriging integrates geochemistry, mineralogy, and structural data to refine the model. Simulation methods generate multiple realisations to quantify uncertainty in grade, tonnage, and mineralogical distribution.

Ore evaluation includes rigorous mineral deportment studies that quantify how rare earths partition into mineral phases and how those phases respond to liberation, flotation, leaching, and separation. Deportment analysis links bench scale results with block models to predict recovery by domain. Deposits with multiple mineral hosts require domain specific processing conditions. Deposits with single dominant mineral hosts deliver higher consistency. Deportment modelling identifies potential losses through slime production, refractory mineral domains, impurity phases, or mineral inclusions.

Economic modelling requires integration of geological data with mining schedules, processing flowsheets, reagent consumption, energy demand, and waste management plans. Engineers calculate net smelter return per tonne, operating cost per tonne, capital intensity, and discounted cash flow metrics. Rare earth projects introduce additional complexity because separation cost varies by element. Dysprosium and terbium require extensive extraction stages, while cerium and lanthanum require simpler circuits. Ore evaluation must account for market value, separation difficulty, and forecast demand for each element. Deposits with a high proportion of magnets elements hold superior economic quality.

Environmental evaluation forms another component of ore assessment. Leaching residues may contain thorium, uranium, fluorine, or sulphate species that require encapsulation and long term monitoring. Tailings storage requires engineered barriers, seepage control, and water treatment. Environmental risk increases cost and influences project timeline. Ore evaluation incorporates these requirements into cost models. Deposits with low radiological load or benign gangue minerals offer reduced environmental liability. Environmental complexity reduces ore quality even when geological grades remain high.

Infrastructure analysis assesses proximity to water, power, chemical supply, ports, and labour. Deposits near existing industrial zones offer reduced logistic cost. Remote deposits require heavy investment in access roads, transmission lines, water pipelines, or accommodation facilities. Ore evaluation includes sensitivity analysis for fuel price, transport cost, and reagent availability. Infrastructure constraints can downgrade otherwise promising deposits.

Processing risk assessment identifies critical technical uncertainties. These include uncertainty in liberation size, sensitivity to grinding, stability of flotation reagents, roasting behaviour, silica gel formation in eudialyte leaching, impurity carryover into pregnant leach solution, and organic phase degradation in solvent extraction. Pilot scale trials reduce this uncertainty. Deposits that deliver predictable processing behaviour under variable conditions achieve higher ore quality classification.

Final ore evaluation consolidates geological, metallurgical, environmental, and economic data into a feasibility framework. High quality deposits demonstrate strong grade continuity, favourable mineralogy, low impurity load, and alignment with proven processing technology. Low quality deposits show complex mineralogy, irregular geometry, high impurity concentration, or unfavourable infrastructure. This evaluation determines whether a deposit advances into mine development or remains a geological prospect.

3.2 Open-pit and underground mining

Mining method selection for rare earth deposits depends on geometry, depth, rock competence, grade distribution, weathering profile, hydrogeology, and geotechnical stability. Rare earth deposits vary widely, from near surface weathered carbonatites to deep high grade veins, and each requires a distinct engineering approach. Open pit mining dominates global production because most economic rare earth deposits occur at shallow to moderate depths with broad lateral extent. Underground mining remains limited to steeply dipping veins, narrow high grade bodies, or deposits beneath prohibitive overburden. The mining method directly influences dilution, recovery, operating cost, waste generation, and environmental footprint.

Open pit mining suits carbonatite systems such as Bayan Obo, Mountain Pass, Mount Weld, and Ngualla because ore bodies display wide footprints, near surface exposure, and predictable geometry. Engineers design pits with phased pushbacks, haul ramps, and geotechnical benches based on rock mass rating, uniaxial compressive strength, joint spacing, and groundwater conditions. Rock strength influences bench height and slope design. Weak weathered carbonatite requires reduced bench heights and flatter slopes. Competent fresh carbonatite supports steeper slopes. Slope stability models incorporate kinematic analysis, shear strength parameters, and groundwater pressure. Dewatering systems, including vertical bores and horizontal drains, control pore pressure and maintain slope integrity.

Open pit operations rely on drilling and blasting to fragment both ore and waste. Blast design depends on rock hardness, mineralogy, and structural fabric. Carbonatite with variable layering requires differential charge distribution to maintain consistent fragmentation. Alkaline intrusive rocks with silicate gangue require higher powder factors due to increased hardness. Engineers monitor vibration, burden relief, and fragmentation curves to optimise recovery. Excavators load material onto haul trucks for transport to crushers or stockpiles. Selective mining reduces dilution when ore boundaries display sharp grade contrasts. Grade control geologists use blast hole assays, X-ray fluorescence, and spectral scanning to delineate ore blocks in real time. Accurate grade control improves recovery and reduces processing of waste.

Underground mining becomes necessary when ore bodies extend below economic pit limits or occur as narrow steeply dipping zones. Underground access uses declines or vertical shafts depending on depth and production rate. Declines suit moderate depths and flexible development. Shafts suit large tonnage operations with high vertical extent. Underground methods include long hole stoping, cut-and-fill, room-and-pillar, shrinkage stoping, and sublevel caving. Method selection depends on ore thickness, dip angle, rock mass rating, and economic cut off grade. Long hole stoping suits steep narrow carbonatite veins in competent rock. Cut-and-fill suits irregular high grade zones where minimising dilution is critical. Room-and-pillar suits shallow, flat, thick bodies as seen in some weathered rare earth rich layers.

Ground support forms a critical component of underground operations. Rock bolts, mesh, shotcrete, and cable bolts stabilise openings based on rock mass classification systems such as Q and RMR. Weak carbonate and altered rocks require heavy support. Hydrothermal alteration zones introduce clay minerals that reduce rock strength and increase swelling. Ventilation systems maintain air quality and remove dust, diesel emissions, and radon associated with thorium or uranium impurities. Underground operations require continuous air monitoring due to radiological exposure risk.

Mining dilution remains a key factor in underground rare earth extraction. Narrow vein systems such as xenotime rich structures display steep grade gradients. Excess waste inclusion reduces head grade and increases processing cost. Engineers use precise drilling, controlled blasting, and backfill placement to limit dilution. Paste backfill supports stope stability and allows pillar recovery, increasing extraction ratio. High backfill strength reduces rock movement in zones with poor ground conditions.

Material handling differs between methods. Open pit mines use large haul trucks and conveyors. Underground mines use load haul dump units, ore passes, and skip hoisting. Rare earth ores often display abrasive behaviour due to associated quartz, zircon, or apatite. This increases wear on equipment and influences maintenance scheduling.

Open pit mining produces large volumes of waste rock requiring engineered dumps with drainage control, erosion protection, and geochemical monitoring. Carbonatite waste often contains high carbonate content that neutralises acidity. Monazite rich deposits require radiological controls for waste placement. Underground mining produces less waste but generates tailings requiring backfill or surface storage.

Mining method selection shapes project economics. Open pits deliver high throughput and low operating cost but carry large environmental footprints. Underground mines deliver lower disturbance but higher cost and reduced flexibility. Deposits with favourable geometry and shallow depth achieve superior economic performance through open pit mining. Deep, irregular, or high grade narrow deposits rely on underground methods.

Open pit mining performance depends on bench design, pit optimisation, and geotechnical monitoring. Engineers use Lerchs Grossmann algorithms and nested pit shells to determine economic limits based on ore value, waste stripping, slope parameters, and processing cost. Cut off grade drives pit depth and shapes mine sequencing. Deposits with strong grade continuity support deep pits because consistent ore value offsets rising strip ratios. Deposits with irregular grade distribution require cautious sequencing to avoid premature exposure of high stripping zones. Geotechnical domains define zones with different slope angles based on lithology, alteration, fracturing, and groundwater. Slope stability monitoring uses radar, extensometers, inclinometers, and piezometers to detect movement and pore pressure changes. Real time monitoring allows rapid intervention to prevent wall failure.

Material fragmentation influences processing efficiency. Blast induced micro fracturing supports downstream comminution, reducing energy demand and improving mineral liberation. Carbonatite responds well to controlled blasting, producing uniform fragmentation. Peralkaline and silica rich host rocks resist fragmentation, generating oversize material and increased crushing demand. Engineers adjust hole diameter, burden, spacing, and explosive type to optimise fragmentation curves. Poor fragmentation increases mine to mill cost and reduces overall recovery. Digital fragmentation analysis using drone imaging or high resolution cameras assists optimisation.

Haulage efficiency determines open pit productivity. Fleet size, haul road gradient, rolling resistance, and truck loading influence cost. Deposits with steep pit walls require longer haulage routes, increasing cycle time. In pit crushing and conveying systems reduce haulage distance and lower fuel use. This method suits large tonnage deposits with consistent geometry. Autonomous haulage systems increase safety and reduce operating cost but require digital infrastructure and high initial capital.

Underground mining requires precise control of stope design, drilling accuracy, and backfill performance. Long hole stoping relies on accurate drill hole placement, straightness, and deviation control to maintain stope walls and limit dilution. Deviated holes increase overbreak and reduce ore value. Engineers use deviation measurement tools and collaring templates to improve accuracy. Sublevel spacing reflects ore thickness, rock strength, and fragmentation requirements. Stope sequencing follows crown pillar stability models that prevent collapse and ensure safe extraction.

Cut and fill mining suits irregular ore shapes and weak ground. Ore is removed in horizontal slices and backfilled with cemented fill or waste rock. Backfill provides local ground support and allows extraction of adjacent slices. This method reduces dilution and maintains grade. Its drawback is slower production and higher cost. Rare earth veins in altered rocks or weathered zones often require cut and fill to maintain wall stability.

Room and pillar mining suits tabular deposits with moderate thickness. Engineers design pillars to maintain roof stability based on rock mass rating and stress field. Pillar recovery occurs only after backfilling. Some rare earth rich saprolite zones in weathered carbonatites may suit modified room and pillar methods with low equipment weight due to soft ground conditions.

Sublevel caving suits large deposits with weak host rock but introduces high dilution. Rare earth mineralisation often occurs in competent rock, reducing suitability for caving. However, caving may apply to altered carbonatite or breccia zones where rock strength decreases. Dilution risk limits adoption of caving in rare earth mining due to the steep drop in head grade that follows mixing with barren material.

Ventilation design remains critical for underground operations. Diesel particulates, dust, and radon from thorium or uranium present major hazards. Ventilation networks require fresh air intakes, exhaust shafts, auxiliary fans, regulators, and monitoring. Airflow models consider pressure losses, airway roughness, heat load, and gas emission rates. Ventilation on demand systems reduce energy use by adjusting airflow according to real time occupancy.

Water control influences underground mine safety and cost. Carbonatites, granites, and altered rocks may host fractured aquifers. Grouting, drainage galleries, and dewatering bores reduce inflows. Water chemistry affects corrosion rate and equipment life. High sulphate or chloride levels require protective coatings. Water inflow increases pumping cost and influences mine design.

Backfill design determines long term stability. Cemented paste fill uses dewatered tailings mixed with binder and water to fill voids. Fill strength depends on binder percentage, curing time, and tailings particle size. Strong fill allows higher extraction ratios by reducing the need for permanent pillars. Backfill quality control includes slump tests, curing tests, compressive strength tests, and binder optimisation.

Mining method selection must account for radiological considerations. Monazite rich underground deposits require increased monitoring due to thorium and uranium. Shielding measures, ventilation, and dust control reduce exposure. Radiological compliance increases cost but remains essential for safe operation.

Open pit and underground methods reflect tradeoffs between cost, safety, productivity, and ore geometry. Rare earth deposits require tailored mining strategies that maintain grade, limit dilution, and support efficient downstream processing.

Mining method effectiveness depends on how ore geometry, geomechanics, and downstream processing interact across the full extraction chain. Rare earth projects emphasise early mine planning because grade distribution and mineralogy determine the correct balance between selectivity, throughput, and operating cost. Open pit and underground options must integrate geostatistical grade models, dilution control, equipment selection, and life of mine sequencing.

Open pit systems achieve highest productivity when ore shows broad lateral extent with moderate dip and shallow depth. Pit shells evolve through iterative optimisation that incorporates updated block models, operational cost, wall angles, and market forecasts for individual rare earth elements. Optimisation must account for heavy rare earth distribution because ore blocks with high dysprosium or terbium content may carry greater strategic value than overall grade suggests. Mine planners use nested pits to compare alternative scenarios under varying strip ratios and price assumptions. High confidence domains with well constrained mineralogy support aggressive pushbacks, while uncertain domains require conservative expansion. Blasting, excavation, and haulage plans must reflect mineralogical heterogeneity. Zones with bastnäsite dominant mineralogy allow rapid movement through crushers. Zones with monazite and xenotime require tighter control due to radiological handling protocols.

Pit dewatering influences geotechnical conditions and mining rate. Rare earth deposits in weathered profiles often contain perched water tables, clay seams, and fractured zones that increase pore pressure and reduce slope stability. Engineers use hydrogeological models to predict inflows and design depressurisation systems. Inflow affects haul road stability and may cause local failures if not monitored continuously. Dewatering reduces energy consumption during crushing because dry ore flows better through primary crushers.

Underground systems focus on controlling dilution while achieving sufficient production rates. Dilution directly reduces feed grade and increases processing cost, especially for deposits with narrow high grade horizons containing xenotime or monazite. Drilling accuracy forms a central control point. Deviation increases when drilling through altered rocks, broken ground, or magnetite rich zones. Anti deviation tools, collar stabilisation, and directional surveys reduce error. If dilution enters the mill feed, mineralogical variation increases variability in leach recovery, solvent extraction performance, and impurity carryover.

Ground conditions determine support requirements. Rare earth deposits often contain alteration halos with clay minerals, carbonate veins, and breccia textures, each affecting rock mass strength. Engineers classify ground according to RMR and Q systems, then install rock bolts, mesh, and shotcrete according to stability models. Support density increases near thorium rich zones because radiological exposure protocols limit worker exposure time, making stable headings essential to reduce repeat entry. Weak hanging walls may require cable bolting or cement reinforced pillars to prevent collapse.

Backfill quality influences long term extraction. Paste fill made from tailings must achieve sufficient strength to support adjacent stopes and allow mining of pillar material. Binder dosage optimisation requires balancing cost with mechanical performance. Binder reactivity may vary according to tailings mineralogy. Rare earth tailings containing fluoride, phosphate, or sulphate impurities may affect curing time and final compressive strength. Underground mines with consistent backfill performance achieve higher extraction ratios and reduced dilution.

Ventilation and air control remain critical because rare earth ores often contain trace thorium and uranium. Dust control must be strict because fine mineral particles transport radionuclides. Engineers use water sprays, foggers, and enclosed transfer points. Real time radiation sensors monitor exposure. Ventilation models incorporate diesel particulate emissions from equipment, heat load from machinery, and radon emission from broken ground. Resistant monazite zones may require additional ventilation capacity due to elevated thorium decay products. Ventilation on demand systems reduce energy cost but require accurate tracking of worker location and airflow requirements.

Underground material handling systems must consider abrasion and corrosive behaviour. Rare earth ores with high quartz or zircon content wear down steel liners and crusher components. High chloride environments in some peralkaline systems cause corrosion. Engineers specify corrosion resistant alloys, ceramic liners, and protective coatings. Bulk flow assessments ensure ore passes and bins avoid hang up due to clay content or moisture. Moisture influenced flow behaviour complicates ore handling in ion adsorption clay systems, requiring moisture control before milling.

Backfill, ventilation, drilling, and ground control come together to define underground cost profile. Open pit mining remains favourable for most rare earth systems, yet underground methods provide access to deeper, higher grade zones where selective extraction is required to maintain economic performance. Final mining method selection reflects cost, safety, geomechanics, processing constraints, and life of mine strategy.

3.3 Beneficiation processes

Beneficiation processes concentrate rare earth minerals from ore by exploiting differences in density, magnetic response, surface chemistry, and particle behaviour. Rare earth deposits present complex mineral associations, variable grain size, and mixed gangue, which demand tailored flowsheets. Beneficiation performance controls downstream leaching efficiency, reagent consumption, and overall project viability. Each mineralogical domain requires specific comminution, classification, and separation strategies that maximise liberation and reject gangue without excessive fines generation.

Comminution forms the first stage of beneficiation. Crushing and grinding aim to liberate bastnäsite, monazite, xenotime, and eudialyte from gangue. Carbonatite hosted minerals usually liberate at moderate grind sizes due to softer carbonate matrix, while silicate rich alkaline and peralkaline systems require finer grinding. Engineers model breakage behaviour using Bond work index tests, SAG mill comminution tests, and mineral liberation analysis. Excessive grinding generates slimes that reduce flotation recovery and increase losses. Optimised comminution balances liberation with particle size control to prevent over milling. Closed circuit grinding with hydrocyclones ensures stable particle size distribution. Screen classification supplements cyclone circuits when clay content or weathered material disrupts hydraulic separation.

Gravity separation applies to placer deposits and some hard rock systems where rare earth minerals show density contrast against quartz or feldspar. Spirals, shaking tables, multi gravity separators, and dense media circuits recover monazite and xenotime from heavy mineral sands. Gravity methods provide high rejection of light gangue, although they perform poorly on fine particles. Electrostatic separation enhances recovery where conductivity differences allow separation of monazite and xenotime from ilmenite, rutile, and zircon.

Magnetic separation targets paramagnetic rare earth minerals and associated iron oxides. Bastnäsite, monazite, and xenotime display weak to moderate magnetic response. High intensity magnetic separators and rare earth roll separators remove magnetic gangue and upgrade concentrate. In carbonatite systems, magnetic separation removes magnetite before flotation, reducing reagent consumption. In heavy mineral sands, rare earth roll separators distinguish monazite and xenotime based on magnetic susceptibility. Magnetic circuits require precise control of feed moisture, particle size, and belt speed to maintain selectivity.

Flotation remains the core beneficiation method for most hard rock rare earth deposits. It exploits differences in surface chemistry between rare earth minerals and gangue. Bastnäsite responds to fatty acids, hydroxamic acids, and modified hydroxamic collectors that form chelated complexes with rare earth ions on mineral surfaces. Monazite and xenotime respond to hydroxamic acids and phosphoric acid esters. Carbonate gangue competes for collectors and requires depressants such as sodium silicate, lignin sulphonate, or citric acid. Conditioning time, pH, reagent dosage, and temperature influence selectivity. Silicate gangue requires dispersants and dispersive grinding conditions. Frother selection influences bubble size distribution and recovery of fine particles. Controlled aeration ensures stable froth structure. Optimised flotation circuits achieve high concentrate grades with moderate recovery, although losses occur in slimes and intergrowths.

Roasting and calcination support beneficiation when fluorine rich minerals or carbonate matrices hinder flotation or leaching. Calcination decomposes bastnäsite into oxides, releasing CO_2 and altering surface chemistry to improve flotation. Roasting removes fluorine species, converts carbonate gangue, and enhances liberation. Thermal treatment must consider energy cost, off gas treatment, and risk of forming refractory phases. Controlled atmosphere roasting prevents oxidation of associated impurities that may hinder downstream processes.

Beneficiation depends heavily on mineralogy. Bastnäsite rich ores produce high grade concentrates with moderate effort. Monazite rich ores require radiological controls. Eudialyte rich ores challenge beneficiation due to fine intergrowths with feldspar and other silicates. Weathered carbonatite profiles produce secondary minerals that respond differently to flotation and require tailored reagent regimes. Clay rich ores generate slimes that reduce recovery without dispersants or pre concentration steps.

Beneficiation defines the feed quality for hydrometallurgical circuits. High quality concentrate reduces acid consumption, increases recovery, and stabilises solvent extraction. Poor beneficiation increases downstream cost and reduces overall yield. Rare earth projects succeed only with beneficiation systems that match mineralogical domains precisely.

Beneficiation performance depends on precise control of particle behaviour and surface chemistry across multiple stages. Each separation stage must address mineralogical complexity, impurity phases, and textural variation. Process engineers design flowsheets that incorporate selective liberation, efficient classification, and reagent regimes matched to mineral surfaces. The objective is to produce a concentrate with stable composition, high rare earth grade, and predictable leachability.

Liberation control relies on advanced mineralogical tools. Automated mineralogy, scanning electron microscopy, and liberation analysis quantify grain size, texture, and mineral association. These tools identify refractory domains, mixed liberation textures, and locked grains that reduce recovery. Liberation curves inform grinding targets. Coarse liberation zones allow reduced energy consumption. Fine intergrowths require selective liberation techniques. High pressure grinding rolls reduce over grinding by applying inter particle breakage. Stirred media mills generate fine particles with narrow size distribution for complex mineral assemblages. Engineers adjust residence time and media characteristics based on mineral hardness and fracture patterns.

Classification determines particle distribution feeding flotation. Hydrocyclones split particles by size and density, yet cyclone inefficiency produces misplaced fines or coarse particles. Clay rich ores increase cyclone bypass and reduce classification accuracy. Engineers use desliming stages to remove ultrafines that reduce flotation selectivity. Reflux classifiers and teeter bed separators improve classification in ores with broad density distribution. Fine particles entering flotation require modified reagent regimes because surface area, charge density, and bubble attachment differ from coarse particles. Flotation optimisation requires understanding of collector adsorption mechanisms. Hydroxamic acids chelate rare earth ions at the mineral surface. Chemisorption varies with pH, ionic strength, and mineral surface oxidation. Carbonate gangue consumes collectors through non specific adsorption. Depressant selection reduces gangue flotation. Sodium silicate modifies surface charge of silicate gangue, preventing attachment. Organic depressants such as starch derivatives reduce froth stability of unwanted minerals. Reagent mixing, conditioning time, and pH control influence collector distribution. Engineers design multi stage rougher scavenger cleaner circuits to improve grade and recovery. Bubble dynamics influence flotation efficiency. Frother selection affects bubble size distribution and froth mobility. Aliphatic alcohols create stable froths suitable for fine particle recovery. Excess frother increases entrainment and gangue carryover. Air rate control adjusts froth depth and residence time. Column flotation increases selectivity through counter current wash water that removes entrained gangue. Microbubble generators improve flotation of ultrafine rare earth particles. Air sparging systems must avoid scale formation, especially in deposits with high carbonate or phosphate content.

Magnetic separation supports flotation by removing magnetic gangue or upgrading specific minerals. Rare earth roll separators distinguish monazite, xenotime, and zircon based on magnetic susceptibility. High gradient magnetic separators capture fine paramagnetic minerals in slimes. Magnetic separation reduces reagent consumption by removing iron bearing minerals that interfere with flotation. Feed moisture, particle shape, and belt cleanliness influence separation effectiveness.

Electrostatic separation remains relevant for heavy mineral sands. Conductivity differences allow separation of monazite and xenotime from ilmenite, rutile, and zircon. Feed must be dry and maintain consistent particle size. This method produces high purity concentrates when combined with magnetic separation.

Chemical pre treatment improves beneficiation in complex ores. Thermal decomposition of bastnäsite alters surface charge and improves collector uptake. Caustic cracking of monazite liberates rare earth phosphates and reduces thorium mobility. Chloride activation of eudialyte produces more reactive mineral surfaces. Pre treatment must consider energy cost, reagent availability, and potential formation of refractory phases.

Process water chemistry influences beneficiation. High carbonate water reduces collector adsorption on bastnäsite. High chloride water affects reagent solubility. Water recirculation requires strict control of dissolved solids to prevent froth instability or collector precipitation. Water treatment using lime, precipitation tanks, or ion exchange ensures consistent process chemistry.

Beneficiation must adapt to mineralogical domains within the same deposit. Carbonatite cores respond differently from weathered zones. Alkaline intrusive rocks differ from hydrothermal veins. Domain specific flowsheets may be required to maintain recovery. Blending strategies reduce variability and stabilise plant performance.

Beneficiation integrates mineralogy, chemistry, and engineering. Successful projects rely on precise control of liberation, flotation, magnetic separation, and water chemistry to create concentrates suited for hydrometallurgical extraction.

Beneficiation effectiveness depends on the stability of the flowsheet under variable feed conditions. Rare earth ores show strong heterogeneity because mineral assemblages, grain size, oxidation state, and gangue composition change across lithological domains, weathering zones, and structural corridors. A beneficiation plant must remain robust against this variability. Process engineers develop adaptive strategies using domain blending, real time monitoring, and dynamic reagent control to stabilise recovery and maintain concentrate quality.

Domain blending smooths mineralogical differences across the feed. Engineers classify ore into domains based on mineralogy, grade, and texture. Blending reduces spikes in clay content, carbonate concentration, or refractory phases. Stable feed allows predictable flotation and lowers reagent cost. Without blending, complex ores create instability in pulp rheology, bubble attachment, and froth structure. Bastnäsite rich zones require different reagent systems than monazite rich zones. Xenotime rich domains require different pH windows and depressants. Blending ensures that plant circuits operate within the optimal performance range.

Real time monitoring strengthens beneficiation control. Online X ray fluorescence units measure rare earth grade, calcium, iron, silica, and phosphate levels in real time. Laser induced breakdown spectroscopy probes mineralogical transitions quickly. Online particle size analysers ensure correct cyclone performance. Froth cameras monitor froth depth, velocity, bubble size, and colour. Machine learning models correlate visual froth features with recovery, allowing autonomous adjustments. Real time magnetic susceptibility sensors monitor feed composition in magnetic circuits. These tools allow rapid correction before instability spreads through the circuit.

Reagent optimisation forms a major factor in beneficiation quality. Collector performance depends on reagent purity, temperature, pH, ionic strength, and dissolved species in process water. Process engineers adjust collector concentration in response to mineralogical changes. Depressants require precise control to suppress carbonate or silicate gangue. Excess depressant reduces rare earth recovery. Frother concentration influences froth mobility, bubble coalescence, and entrainment. Domain specific reagent recipes emerge through locked cycle tests. Plants with automated reagent addition systems maintain stable performance across varying feed conditions.

Deleterious elements influence beneficiation performance. High iron content saturates magnetic separation circuits and increases reagent consumption. High fluorine content alters bubble formation and may reduce collector adsorption. Phosphorus modifies surface charge and increases scale formation in conditioning tanks. Carbonate gangue raises pH and increases lime consumption. Sulphate bearing minerals influence redox potential. Beneficiation strategies must identify and manage deleterious elements through selective removal, water treatment, or modified reagent schemes.

Slime management remains critical because ultrafine particles cause entrainment, reduce selectivity, and impair filtration. Slimes originate from weathered carbonatite, clay rich horizons, and grinding of brittle gangue. Desliming using hydrocyclones, centrifuges, or hydraulic classifiers reduces slime load entering flotation. Flocculants and dispersants modify slime behaviour. Poor slime control reduces plant stability and increases losses of rare earths within fine gangue fractions. Tailings dewatering requires thickening, flocculation, and filter presses. Slurry rheology affects pump performance and pipeline friction losses. Process integration influences beneficiation success. Grinding, classification, flotation, magnetic separation, and dewatering must operate in harmony. A change in one stage propagates downstream. Increased fines from grinding alter flotation performance. Excess slimes from weathered ore zones impair magnetic separation. Process engineers use mass balance models, circuit simulations, and pilot scale tests to optimise flowsheets. Plants often incorporate recirculation streams, scavenger flotation, and regrind mills to recover lost minerals. Stable integration reduces operational risk.

Waste management influences beneficiation economics. Tailings contain residual reagents, dissolved salts, radionuclides, and fine mineral particles. Tailings storage facilities require engineered embankments, seepage control, and water recycling. Water reclaimed from tailings influences process chemistry. Plants must control dissolved solids, hardness, pH, and ionic strength. Poor water quality reduces collector efficiency, disrupts flotation, and increases scaling. Water treatment using precipitation, lime addition, and clarifiers maintains stable water chemistry.

Beneficiation quality defines hydrometallurgical performance. High rare earth grade, low impurity concentrate reduces acid consumption and improves leach kinetics. Concentrates with high carbonate, silicate, or phosphate content require higher reagent use and may form refractory residues. Consistent concentrate quality reduces variability in solvent extraction circuits and improves predictability of separation performance. Beneficiation therefore acts as the gatekeeper for the entire rare earth value chain.

3.4 Hydrometallurgical and pyrometallurgical separation
Hydrometallurgical and pyrometallurgical separation form the core of rare earth refining because rare earth minerals display strong lattice stability, similar trivalent chemistry, and narrow ionic radius differences. Effective separation requires controlled decomposition of mineral lattices, dissolution of rare earths into selective leach media, removal of impurities, and multi stage isolation of individual elements.

Each step must account for mineralogy, gangue chemistry, redox behaviour, and reagent stability.

Hydrometallurgical processing begins with mineral decomposition. Bastnäsite requires calcination to remove CO_2 and fluorine species. Calcination at controlled temperatures converts fluorocarbonates into oxides, modifies surface chemistry, and improves acid solubility. Monazite requires aggressive digestion because its phosphate lattice resists leaching. Sulphuric acid digestion at high temperature breaks phosphate bonds and releases rare earth sulphates. This step generates thorium and uranium rich residues that require controlled neutralisation and permanent storage. Xenotime undergoes similar sulphate digestion but demands higher temperatures due to tight lattice structure. Eudialyte requires chloride based leaching because sulphate and nitrate leaching trigger silica gel formation that clogs equipment and lowers recovery. Chloride leaching dissolves rare earths while stabilising silica in soluble complexes or controlled precipitates.

Leach liquor preparation requires removal of impurities such as iron, aluminium, calcium, magnesium, silica, and thorium. Precipitation methods adjust pH to remove iron and aluminium as hydroxides. Rare earths remain in solution due to their lower hydrolysis tendency at controlled pH. Calcium and magnesium require selective reagents or temperature control to prevent co precipitation. Silica requires careful handling through magnesium induced coagulation or controlled polymer stabilisation. Thorium removal requires precise pH and redox conditions to ensure quantitative precipitation without rare earth loss. Failure to stabilise impurities disrupts downstream solvent extraction and reduces phase stability.

Solvent extraction forms the backbone of hydrometallurgical separation. Rare earth ions form inner sphere complexes with organophosphorus extractants such as tributyl phosphate, di(2 ethylhexyl) phosphoric acid, and phosphinic acids. Distribution coefficients rise across the rare earth series due to increasing charge density and decreasing ionic radius. This behaviour allows stepwise separation using counter current mixer settler trains with hundreds of stages. Extraction circuits separate light and heavy groups first, then isolate individual elements through progressively refined extractant strength, acidity, and phase composition. Organic phase stability remains critical because extractant degradation, third phase formation, and emulsification disrupt separation. Engineers maintain strict control of pH, phase ratio, and temperature to stabilise extraction profiles. Ion exchange complements solvent extraction when high purity heavy rare earth fractions require finer separation resolution.

Pyrometallurgical separation supports hydrometallurgy by producing intermediate compounds or metals. High temperature chlorination converts rare earth oxides into rare earth chlorides. These chlorides exhibit improved volatility and enhanced separation selectivity. Controlled chlorination requires inert atmospheres to prevent oxidation and volatilisation of impurities. Metallothermic reduction using calcium or lithium produces rare earth metals from chlorides. Reduction reactions follow thermodynamic gradients where strong reductants capture chlorine, leaving metallic lanthanides. Electrolytic reduction of rare earth chlorides offers higher purity but requires corrosion resistant cells, oxygen free atmospheres, and precise control of current density.

Pyrometallurgical roasting modifies mineral structures during pre treatment. Fluorine bearing bastnäsite decomposes to oxides, reducing reagent consumption in leaching. Phosphate decomposition during monazite roasting increases reactivity. Alkaline fusion using sodium hydroxide or sodium carbonate cracks silicate structures in eudialyte and allanite. Fusion converts rare earths into water soluble species and separates silica as an insoluble phase. Fusion remains energy intensive but enables processing of mineralogies unsuitable for direct acid leaching.

Hydrometallurgical and pyrometallurgical separation depend on impurity control because impurities follow similar chemical pathways. Thorium and uranium require strict management due to radiological hazards. Iron, aluminium, and manganese alter extractant behaviour and reduce selectivity. Fluorine influences roasting gas quality and corrodes equipment. Successful separation arises from stable mineral decomposition, controlled leaching, impurity removal, and precise solvent extraction.

These processes transform mineral concentrates into purified rare earth solutions or oxides. The next stages refine these products into individual high purity materials used in magnets, catalysts, optics, and electronics. Hydrometallurgical separation depends on precise control of chemical conditions that govern dissolution kinetics, impurity behaviour, complex formation, and phase transfer. Each mineral class presents characteristic challenges that shape reagent selection, reactor design, and downstream separation strategy.

Leaching kinetics reflect mineral crystallography and surface accessibility. Bastnäsite decomposition after calcination follows proton attack on oxide surfaces. Reaction rates depend on temperature, acid concentration, dissolved CO_2, and the presence of secondary phases. Monazite digestion follows phosphate breakdown and forms rare earth sulphates with intermediate thorium and uranium complexes. This process requires temperatures above two hundred degrees Celsius and high sulphuric acid concentration to maintain reaction rate. Xenotime digestion mirrors monazite behaviour but demands longer residence times. Eudialyte leaching under chloride systems requires chloride rich solutions at elevated temperature. Silica control dominates because uncontrolled polymerisation produces gels that immobilise rare earths. Engineers add aluminium chloride, magnesium chloride, or other silica modifiers to inhibit polymer growth.

Impurity management remains crucial. Iron precipitates as hydroxide at controlled pH values, but co precipitation of rare earths must be avoided. Aluminium, manganese, and titanium interfere with solvent extraction and must be removed during pre treatment. Sulphate complexes alter extraction patterns and require neutralisation steps. Fluoride forms stable complexes with heavy rare earths and influences phase transfer. Calcium and magnesium increase reagent consumption and scale formation. Impurity control relies on pH adjustment, seed precipitation, oxidation reduction control, and selective complexants.

Solvent extraction forms the most significant stage in hydrometallurgy due to the chemical similarity of rare earths. Distribution coefficients vary systematically across the lanthanide series, increasing from light to heavy. This trend allows separation through staged extraction. Engineers design multi bank circuits with hundreds of mixer settlers. Each stage transfers a fraction of rare earths into the organic phase depending on acidity, extractant concentration, organic to aqueous phase ratio, and temperature. Counter current flow improves efficiency. Scrubbing stages remove impurities that follow rare earths. Stripping stages regenerate aqueous rare earth streams for further purification. Phase continuity must remain stable. Organic phase degradation produces phosphoric acid or polymerised products that reduce extraction efficiency. Third phase formation occurs when overloaded organic phase splits into two organic layers, disrupting separation. Engineers monitor interfacial tension, phase disengagement time, and emulsion stability to prevent failure.

Ion exchange supports refinement of heavy rare earth elements where narrow separation factors require high resolution. Strong acid cation resins, chelating resins, and nanostructured resins adsorb rare earth ions based on charge density, hydration behaviour, and complexation strength. Elution gradients isolate individual rare earths. Ion exchange suits low volume, high purity production rather than bulk separation.

Pyrometallurgical routes complement hydrometallurgy by producing metals or intermediate products. Rare earth chlorides produced through high temperature chlorination display higher volatility and improved separation. Chlorination reagents include chlorine gas, ammonium chloride, and carbon tetrachloride. These processes require inert atmospheres to prevent oxidation. Fluidised bed reactors support uniform temperature distribution. Chlorination breaks down refractory phases, allowing subsequent separation by distillation or fractional sublimation. Metallothermic reduction produces rare earth metals by reacting rare earth chlorides with calcium or lithium. Reduction requires molten salt flux, inert gas shielding, and precise temperature control. Metal product must be protected from oxygen and nitrogen contamination.

Vacuum distillation and sublimation separate rare earth halides and metals based on vapour pressure differences. Heavy rare earths display lower vapour pressures and require higher temperatures. Light rare earths volatilise more readily. Distillation occurs under controlled vacuum to prevent oxidation. Condensation surfaces collect purified fractions.

Pyrometallurgical separation requires careful management of fluorine, chlorine, and sulphur bearing gases. Gas cleaning systems use scrubbers, absorbers, and filters to meet emission standards. Refractory linings must resist corrosion. Energy input remains high, but pyrometallurgy provides pathways not accessible through hydrometallurgy alone, particularly for metal production and purification.

Hydrometallurgical and pyrometallurgical routes integrate in advanced plants. Hydrometallurgy generates purified oxides. Pyrometallurgy converts oxides to metals or alloys. The interface between these routes defines overall refining efficiency and product purity. Separation success requires detailed understanding of mineralogy, aqueous chemistry, high temperature thermodynamics, and impurity control.

Hydrometallurgical and pyrometallurgical separation demand integrated process control because rare earth chemistry remains sensitive to small variations in pH, redox potential, ionic strength, and temperature. Refining circuits must maintain consistent operating conditions across numerous reactors, settlers, and furnaces. Instability in one stage propagates through the entire system and reduces product purity. Engineers apply multivariable control systems, automated sampling, and predictive modelling to stabilise extraction, impurity removal, and phase transitions.

In hydrometallurgy, leaching reactors require strict monitoring of acid concentration, temperature, and slurry density. Temperature influences dissolution kinetics, impurity solubility, and silica behaviour. Excess temperature accelerates silica polymerisation in eudialyte leaching, forming gels that trap rare earths. Insufficient temperature slows monazite digestion and reduces sulphate formation. Agitation influences mass transfer and prevents local concentration gradients. Slurry density affects residence time and heat transfer. Engineers apply continuous temperature measurement, automated acid addition, and density control loops to maintain optimal leaching conditions.

Filtration and solid liquid separation follow leaching. Thickening performance depends on flocculant selection, shear conditions, and particle surface properties. Rare earth slurries often contain fine clay or phosphate particles that resist settling. High solids loading disrupts flocculation. Engineers use high rate thickeners, lamella settlers, or centrifuges to handle difficult slurries. Filtration requires pressure filters, belt filters, or ceramic filters. Filter performance influences downstream solvent extraction by affecting clarity, dissolved solids, and impurity load. Filtrate chemistry must remain within narrow ionic strength and pH limits to avoid extractor instability.

Solvent extraction demands the highest degree of process stability. Extractant concentration must remain constant despite degradation and entrainment losses. Organic loss occurs through entrainment in aqueous phase, volatilisation, or decomposition. Plants use phase separators, coalescers, carbon treatment, and periodic purification to maintain organic integrity. Mixer settler residence time determines phase continuity. Incorrect agitation produces stable emulsions that reduce separation efficiency. Temperature influences distribution coefficients, extractant viscosity, and interfacial tension. Engineers stabilise extraction circuits using closed loop control based on pH probes, flow meters, density sensors, and temperature monitoring. Multi bank circuits with hundreds of stages require coordinated operation to prevent cascading failures.

Stripping and precipitation convert rare earth loaded organic phase back into aqueous phase. Oxalate precipitation remains common because rare earth oxalates form selectively and decompose cleanly upon calcination. Precipitation requires strict pH and reagent control. Impurities such as iron and aluminium co precipitate if conditions shift. Oxalate crystals must achieve specific morphology and purity to support calcination. Calcination converts oxalates to oxides. Temperature ramps must avoid sintering or phase transitions that reduce reactivity.

Pyrometallurgical refining requires control of high temperature reactions. Chlorination of rare earth oxides demands stable temperature profiles, controlled flow of chlorine bearing gases, and uniform contact between solids and gas phase. Reactors require refractory linings resistant to halide corrosion. Gas off streams contain chlorine, hydrogen chloride, and metal halides that require scrubbing and neutralisation. Metallothermic reduction requires molten salt flux with controlled composition to ensure efficient reaction between reductants and rare earth chlorides. Bath composition influences reduction yield, slag formation, and metal purity. Reduction generates heat that must be controlled to prevent runaway reaction.

Distillation and sublimation processes require precise temperature gradients and vacuum regulation. Rare earth halides exhibit varying vapour pressures that govern separation. Temperature too high risks decomposition or contamination. Temperature too low reduces volatility. Vacuum pumps maintain low pressure to enhance volatilisation and limit oxidation. Condensing surfaces collect purified halide fractions that later convert to oxides or metals through additional steps.

Process integration ensures that hydrometallurgical and pyrometallurgical stages operate in sequence. Plants often produce intermediate oxides through hydrometallurgy, then convert oxides to metals through pyrometallurgy. Data from hydrometallurgy informs pyrometallurgical steps. Impurity profiles, rare earth distribution, and moisture content influence reaction behaviour. Advanced plants use digital twins and dynamic simulation to predict performance and identify optimisation scenarios.

Hydrometallurgical and pyrometallurgical separation achieve high purity only through precise chemistry, controlled thermodynamics, and continuous monitoring. These methods enable extraction of rare earths from complex mineral matrices and underpin the global rare earth supply chain.

3.5 Radioactive by-products and handling requirements

Radioactive by products arise from thorium and uranium that substitute for rare earths within phosphate, silicate, and fluorocarbonate lattices. Monazite carries the highest radiological load because thorium occupies lattice sites through coupled substitution. Xenotime often contains uranium and thorium at variable levels. Allanite, zircon, and apatite contain trace radionuclides that accumulate during beneficiation and hydrometallurgy. These impurities migrate into residues, tailings, and process solutions, creating radiological exposure risk and requiring engineering controls throughout mining, beneficiation, and refining.

During mining, radioactive minerals disperse through dust, broken rock, and weathered profiles. Open pit operations generate airborne particulate that contains thorium and uranium. Dust suppression, water sprays, and enclosed transfer points reduce dispersion. Radiological surveys identify hotspots in ore faces and stockpiles. Operators track exposure through dosimetry and air sampling. Underground mines require continuous airflow and radon monitoring due to decay products that accumulate in confined spaces. Ventilation removes radon, thoron, and particulate. Ground control in monazite rich zones must account for increased radiological protocols because workers must spend limited time in high concentration areas.

Beneficiation concentrates radionuclides because monazite and xenotime report to heavy fractions. Gravity separation, magnetic separation, and flotation increase activity concentration in intermediate products. Tailings derived from gangue contain residual radionuclides that require controlled placement. Radiological characterisation defines tailings classification. Engineering controls include lined tailings cells, seepage collection, geotechnical monitoring, and water management systems. Water recirculation must control radionuclide mobility through precipitation, adsorption, and ion exchange. High chloride or low pH water increases uranium mobility and must be stabilised before discharge.

Hydrometallurgical processing concentrates radionuclides in residues. Monazite digestion yields thorium and uranium rich sulphate residues with long half lives. These residues require controlled neutralisation with lime or magnesium oxide to precipitate thorium and uranium as hydroxides. Precipitated material requires encapsulation and placement in engineered repositories. Repositories use clay liners, geomembranes, drainage layers, and capping systems to isolate radioactive residues. Residue storage designs incorporate seismic stability, groundwater modelling, and long term settlement analysis. Uranium in solution requires reduction and precipitation to limit mobility. Thorium requires precise pH control to ensure quantitative removal without rare earth loss.

Process equipment experiences radiological loading because radionuclides adsorb onto surfaces during digestion, precipitation, or solvent extraction. Equipment decontamination requires acid washing, high pressure water, or alkaline treatment. Decontaminated residues require controlled disposal. Extraction circuits require shielding or remote handling in high activity sections. Radiological control remains essential to protect workers and maintain environmental compliance.

Air emissions require monitoring because roasting and drying equipment may release dust or radon bearing gases. Gas treatment includes bag filters, scrubbers, and activated carbon systems. Stack emissions require continuous monitoring for particulate, thorium, uranium, and decay products. Operators maintain regulatory reporting for emission limits and radiological compliance.

Worker protection demands strict protocols. Personal protective equipment includes respirators, Tyvek suits, gloves, and radiation badges. Access to high activity zones requires rotation schedules, administrative controls, and time limits. Workers receive training on radiological hazards, contamination prevention, and emergency procedures. Health surveillance includes periodic blood tests, lung function tests, and dosimetry review.

Environmental monitoring includes groundwater sampling, surface water analysis, soil testing, and biological monitoring. Sampling frequencies follow radiological licence conditions. Modelling tools predict radionuclide migration under extreme weather, seismic events, or facility failure. Monitoring results inform corrective actions.

Transport of radioactive materials requires specialised containers, labelling, documentation, and regulatory permits. Monazite concentrates and thorium bearing residues fall under transport regulations for radioactive substances. Containers require shielding, impact resistance, and leak prevention. Transport routes must avoid densely populated areas where possible.

Radioactive by products define the engineering and regulatory complexity of rare earth extraction. Effective management requires strict controls across mining, beneficiation, hydrometallurgy, waste storage, and environmental monitoring. These measures ensure compliance, protect workers, and maintain long term environmental safety.

Radioactive by products persist through every stage of rare earth processing because thorium and uranium behave differently from rare earths during mineral decomposition, leaching, and separation. Their distinct chemistry requires targeted removal steps, engineered containment systems, and compliance with radiological standards. The behaviour of radionuclides depends on oxidation state, ligand stability, pH, and redox environment. Uranium occurs as U^{4+} and U^{6+}. Thorium remains almost entirely as Th^{4+}. These oxidation states govern mobility and dictate removal strategy.

Leaching conditions influence radionuclide solubility. Sulphuric acid digestion solubilises most uranium into the leach liquor through formation of UO_2SO_4 complexes, while thorium precipitates at moderate pH due to its strong hydrolysis. Chloride leaching dissolves uranium and thorium variably depending on chloride concentration and redox potential. Nitrate leaching stabilises UO_2^{2+} but leaves Th^{4+} largely insoluble. Engineers design leaching systems to maximise rare earth solubility while controlling radionuclide behaviour. Reducing agents such as ferrous iron or sulphur dioxide convert U^{6+} to U^{4+}, decreasing mobility and enhancing precipitation. Oxidising conditions increase U^{6+} and stabilise soluble complexes. Thorium requires precise addition of neutralising agents such as lime or magnesium hydroxide to precipitate quantitatively.

Residue management forms one of the most critical elements of radioactive handling. Leach residues contain thorium, uranium, and decay products. Residue neutralisation adjusts pH to precipitate radionuclides as hydroxides, carbonates, or mixed phases. Residues undergo thickening, filtration, and drying to reduce moisture content. Dry residues reduce leachate generation and allow stable encapsulation. Encapsulation uses engineered barriers such as cement matrices, polymer coatings, or geopolymer materials. These matrices immobilise radionuclides by physical containment and chemical bonding. Waste forms undergo leach testing, compressive strength testing, and long term stability assessment.

Storage facilities require multi layer barrier systems. Clay liners provide low permeability. Geomembranes prevent percolation. Drainage layers collect seepage. Cover systems prevent infiltration and reduce radon release. Foundations require geotechnical analysis to ensure stability under seismic loading, heavy rainfall, and long term settlement. Facilities incorporate groundwater monitoring wells, leak detection systems, and observation trenches. Storage design must consider the long half lives of thorium decay chains and ensure containment over decades.

Effluent treatment manages radionuclide mobility in process water. Uranium remains soluble under certain pH and redox conditions and requires selective precipitation or ion exchange. Thorium precipitates readily but may redissolve if pH fluctuates. Water treatment trains include neutralisation tanks, clarifiers, ion exchange units, and membrane filtration. Sludge generated from effluent treatment requires classification as radioactive waste and subsequent encapsulation. Discharge water must meet radiological standards that limit alpha and beta activity.

Solvent extraction systems require radiological control because thorium and uranium may follow rare earths into organic phases under specific conditions. Thorium forms complexes with organophosphorus extractants, especially at low acidity. Engineers include guard extraction stages or thorium scrub stages to prevent contamination of rare earth circuits. Organic solvents contaminated with radionuclides require regeneration or disposal under radiological protocols. Extractant degradation products may concentrate radionuclides and require removal to maintain purity.

Dust and airborne contamination require continuous control. Crushing, grinding, flotation, roasting, and drying generate fine particles that contain radionuclides. Industrial hygiene systems use dust suppression sprays, bag filters, cyclones, and negative pressure enclosures. Air monitoring equipment measures alpha, beta, and gamma activity. Ventilation systems remove radon and thoron decay products. Workers must wear respirators and protective clothing in high contamination zones. Dust control reduces inhalation exposure and minimises contamination of equipment.

Radiological monitoring programmes form a core requirement. Workers wear personal dosimeters that record cumulative exposure. Area monitors track airborne activity. Surface contamination meters verify cleanliness of equipment and work areas. Sampling programmes include groundwater, surface water, sediment, soil, and vegetation. Results feed into environmental impact assessments and compliance reporting. Regulatory authorities review monitoring data and enforce corrective actions.

Emergency planning requires identification of potential release scenarios, spill containment procedures, evacuation routes, and decontamination protocols. Facilities must maintain spill response teams trained in radiological hazards. Emergency drills ensure preparedness for incidents involving residue leaks, equipment failure, or containment breach. Long term institutional controls may include land use restrictions, access limitations, and ongoing environmental monitoring.

Radioactive by products require rigorous management because their mobility, radiological hazard, and long half lives generate environmental and operational risk. Successful rare earth operations integrate radiological engineering, chemical control, and regulatory compliance across the entire processing chain.

Radioactive by products impose long term obligations because thorium and uranium decay chains produce alpha, beta, and gamma emissions over extended timescales. Handling requirements must therefore address immediate operational hazards and multi decade stewardship. Engineering design, chemical control, monitoring, and regulatory compliance combine to manage exposure, immobilise radionuclides, and prevent environmental release.

Radiological characterisation identifies activity concentration in ore, concentrates, residues, and tailings. Characterisation requires gamma spectrometry, alpha spectroscopy, and radiochemical analysis to quantify thorium 232, uranium 238, radium 226, and decay products. These measurements classify material under radiological regulations. Ore with low activity may require minimal controls. Concentrates with monazite or xenotime require enhanced controls. Residues with concentrated thorium require engineered containment. Characterisation informs exposure limits, waste classification, and facility design.

Worker exposure control requires management of external dose, inhalation dose, and ingestion dose. External dose arises from gamma emitters. Inhalation dose arises from dust and radon progeny. Ingestion dose arises from contamination on hands or food surfaces. Facilities implement strict hygiene protocols, restricted access zones, controlled changing areas, and contamination monitoring. Personal dosimeters quantify cumulative dose. Workers rotate through tasks to limit high exposure periods. Engineering controls reduce airborne activity through ventilation, dust suppression, and negative pressure containment in critical areas.

Equipment decontamination forms a major requirement because radionuclides adsorb onto steel surfaces, polymer linings, and process vessels. Decontamination methods include acid washing, alkaline flushing, high pressure spraying, and abrasive cleaning. Decontamination fluids require collection, neutralisation, and disposal as radioactive waste. Equipment nearing end of life requires radiological assessment before disposal or recycling. Thick contaminant layers may require encasement of equipment as radioactive waste.

Tailings and residues represent the largest radioactive inventory. Tailings storage facilities require engineered design based on hydrology, geotechnics, and radiological modelling. Facilities use composite liners, leachate collection, embankment stability design, and controlled placement procedures. Tailings must be placed to minimise dust generation and erosion. Cover systems include clay barriers, geomembranes, and vegetative layers. Covers limit radon flux, reduce infiltration, and prevent contact between radionuclides and biota. Monitoring wells measure groundwater quality. Seepage intercept systems capture contaminated water for treatment. Facilities undergo periodic stability assessment and must accommodate long term settlement and climate variability.

Residue repositories for thorium rich waste require enhanced containment. Residues undergo solidification, encapsulation, and packaging into engineered containers. Containers require corrosion resistant materials, radiation shielding, and robust sealing. Repositories must withstand seismic events, extreme weather, and long term subsidence. Institutional control includes land use restrictions, access control, and periodic inspection. Regulatory authorities require financial assurance to maintain repositories after mine closure.

Environmental monitoring addresses air, water, soil, and biological pathways. Air monitoring detects radon, thoron, and particulate. Water monitoring tracks radionuclides in groundwater, rivers, and surface runoff. Soil sampling identifies accumulation around facilities. Biological monitoring tests plants, fish, and wildlife for radionuclide uptake. Monitoring programmes ensure compliance with radiological dose limits for the public and the environment. Data supports adaptive management if anomalies appear.

Transport requirements apply to monazite concentrates, thorium bearing residues, uranium bearing solutions, and contaminated equipment. Transport regulations classify radionuclides, define packaging requirements, and mandate documentation. Packages require shielding, impact resistance, and leak resistance. Transport routes require risk assessment. Drivers require radiological training.

Regulatory compliance requires licensing of mining, beneficiation, hydrometallurgical processing, residue storage, and decommissioning. Regulators review radiological assessments, facility designs, monitoring plans, emergency procedures, and closure plans. Companies must demonstrate ability to manage radionuclides over long timeframes. Closure plans include decommissioning of equipment, remediation of contaminated soil, sealing of repositories, and long term monitoring.

Decommissioning presents unique challenges. Contaminated structures require dismantling under radiological control. Soil remediation requires excavation and segregation of contaminated material.

Equipment requires decontamination or disposal. Tailings and residue facilities require final covers and drainage control. Post closure monitoring ensures continued containment. Financial assurance mechanisms guarantee long term stewardship.

Radioactive by products impose complex operational, environmental, and regulatory demands. Effective management protects workers, communities, and ecosystems. These requirements define the responsible development of rare earth projects.

4. Refining, Metallurgy, and Advanced Processing
4.1 Solvent extraction
Solvent extraction isolates rare earth ions through selective transfer between an aqueous phase and an organic phase containing extractants with strong affinity for trivalent lanthanides. This technique dominates industrial separation because it exploits systematic trends across the lanthanide series, including decreasing ionic radius, increasing charge density, and rising complex stability. The process requires long extraction banks with hundreds of mixer settlers arranged in counter current configuration. Each stage transfers a small fraction of the load, achieving fine elemental resolution when combined across the entire circuit.

Organic extractants define separation performance. Organophosphorus compounds remain standard due to high selectivity for trivalent rare earth ions. Di(2 ethylhexyl) phosphoric acid, mono(2 ethylhexyl) phosphonic acid, and phosphinic acids form inner sphere complexes. Their structure allows deprotonation that creates negatively charged ligands capable of binding rare earth cations. Complexes transfer into the organic phase due to hydrophobic interactions with the solvent. Extractant strength influences distribution coefficients. Strong extractants target heavy rare earths. Weaker extractants favour light rare earths. Process engineers design extractant mixtures to adjust selectivity, phase stability, and resistance to degradation.

Phase composition influences extraction. Organic phase contains extractant, diluent, and modifiers. Diluents include kerosene or refined aliphatic hydrocarbons with low aromatic content to reduce emulsion formation. Modifiers such as long chain alcohols reduce third phase formation by improving interfacial tension. The aqueous phase contains rare earth sulphates, chlorides, or nitrates depending on upstream leaching method. Ionic strength, acidity, and temperature influence extraction performance. High acidity suppresses extraction of light lanthanides. Moderate acidity enhances extraction of heavy lanthanides. Engineers tune acidity to achieve group separation of light, middle, and heavy elements.

Distribution coefficients describe the ratio of rare earth concentration in organic to aqueous phases. These coefficients vary across the lanthanide series. Heavy rare earths show higher coefficients due to stronger ligand binding. Light rare earths show lower coefficients due to weaker ligand interactions. This trend creates natural separation gradients. Engineers arrange mixer settlers to exploit these gradients. Extraction banks remove heavy elements first, leaving light elements in raffinate. Scrubbing banks remove co extracted impurities. Stripping banks return rare earths to aqueous phase using acidic or complexing solutions.

Mixer settlers provide mechanical mixing and rapid phase separation. Mixers disperse aqueous droplets into organic phase, increasing contact surface. Residence time influences extraction completeness. Settlers provide quiet zones where phases separate by gravity. Interfacial behaviour remains critical. Emulsions reduce efficiency and require control through appropriate mixing intensity, temperature, and modifier dosage. Phase continuity determines which phase disperses into the other. Organic continuous systems favour extraction of heavy rare earths. Aqueous continuous systems suit light rare earth stripping. Engineers manage phase continuity to optimise selectivity.

Impurity behaviour affects extraction. Iron, aluminium, titanium, and manganese form complexes that partially follow rare earths. These elements reduce loading capacity, destabilise extractant, and reduce purity. Thorium and uranium require dedicated removal stages because they form stable complexes at moderate acidity. Phosphate, sulphate, and chloride ions influence extractant deprotonation, interfacial tension, and phase separation. Water content in organic phase influences reagent stability and distribution coefficients. Engineers monitor aqueous and organic conductivity, acidity, and impurity profiles continuously.

Phase degradation remains a major operational challenge. Extractants degrade through hydrolysis, oxidation, or thermal decomposition. Degradation products accumulate in both phases, altering interfacial behaviour. This produces third phase formation, increased viscosity, and reduced selectivity. Plants use carbon treatment, re distillation, and phase purification to maintain extractant quality. Organic phase bleed streams remove degraded material and maintain steady state composition.

Temperature influences all extraction parameters. Distribution coefficients rise with temperature for heavy rare earths but may decline for light rare earths depending on extractant structure. Viscosity decreases with heat, improving mass transfer. Excess temperature accelerates degradation. Temperature control stabilises phase behaviour, prevents third phase formation, and improves separation accuracy.

Solvent extraction offers unmatched resolution among rare earth separation techniques. It remains energy efficient compared to pyrometallurgical methods but requires long circuits, precise control, and extensive monitoring. Its success depends on extractant stability, phase management, impurity control, and predictable aqueous chemistry.

Solvent extraction performance depends on mass transfer kinetics, interfacial behaviour, phase composition, and circuit configuration. Engineers design circuits to exploit differences in distribution coefficients across the lanthanide series while managing impurities, preventing instability, and maintaining high throughput. Precise control of extraction, scrubbing, and stripping ensures progressive refinement from mixed rare earth solutions to individual high purity streams.

Mass transfer kinetics govern the rate at which rare earth ions transfer between aqueous and organic phases. Mass transfer occurs through diffusion, film transport, and complex formation at the interface. Droplet size, agitation intensity, and residence time determine overall rate. Smaller droplets increase interfacial surface area but increase entrainment. Excess agitation creates stable emulsions that resist phase separation. Engineers balance agitation to maximise extraction while avoiding emulsion formation. Droplet coalescence in settlers depends on interfacial tension, viscosity, and presence of surfactant impurities. High silica, organic degradation products, or suspended solids reduce coalescence and destabilise phase behaviour. Continuous removal of solids through filtration maintains stability.

Circuit configuration defines extraction sequence. Rare earths separate progressively across three major zones: extraction, scrubbing, and stripping. Extraction loads rare earths into the organic phase. Scrubbing removes co extracted impurities such as iron, aluminium, thorium, or uranium. Stripping regenerates the organic phase by transferring rare earths back into aqueous phase. Each zone uses multiple mixer settlers. Counter current flow reduces reagent use and increases separation efficiency. Organic and aqueous flow rates must remain stable to maintain correct phase ratios. Deviations alter loading, shift equilibrium, and degrade separation.

Extractant concentration influences separation. High concentration increases loading but increases viscosity and slows phase disengagement. Low concentration reduces capacity and increases circuit length. Engineers establish extractant concentration at steady state through solvent make up, bleed streams, and purity control. Diluents control viscosity, flash point, and extraction kinetics. High flash point diluents reduce fire risk but may reduce mass transfer. Low aromatic diluents reduce degradation but increase cost. Solvent systems require strict control of water content because water in organic phase alters acidity and complex stability.

Scrubbing stages represent a major determinant of purity. Scrubbing removes elements that follow rare earths due to similar complexation behaviour. Thorium requires targeted scrubbing at narrow pH ranges. Uranium requires redox control. Iron and aluminium require pH adjustment or complexing agents. Scrubbing must avoid stripping desired rare earths. Engineers adjust acidity, temperature, and scrub reagent concentration to achieve selective removal without degrading loading.

Stripping stages regenerate aqueous streams containing individual rare earth groups. Stripping uses mineral acids, chelating agents, or lower acidity to reverse extraction equilibrium. Light rare earths strip at lower acidity. Heavy rare earths require stronger conditions. Temperature influences stripping kinetics and solubility. Stripping stages determine final concentration and purity of rare earth solutions. These solutions then undergo precipitation or crystallisation to produce oxalates, carbonates, or chlorides.

Phase continuity remains a core operational concern. Organic continuous systems reduce entrainment of aqueous droplets. Aqueous continuous systems reduce organic loss. Phase inversion occurs when phase ratio changes or impurities disrupt interfacial behaviour. Phase inversion reduces capacity, increases losses, and destabilises circuits. Engineers monitor flow rates, phase densities, and interfacial tension to avoid inversion.

Organic management prevents degradation. Extractants degrade through hydrolysis, especially under high acidity. Oxidation occurs at elevated temperature or in presence of oxygen. Degradation reduces selectivity, increases viscosity, and forms surfactants that stabilise emulsions. Plants use activated carbon to remove degradation products. Diluents undergo re distillation to remove volatile contaminants. Regular solvent purification maintains extraction efficiency.

Aqueous chemistry shapes extraction behaviour. Ionic strength modifies activity coefficients. Sulphate or chloride complexes influence extraction selectivity. pH determines extractant deprotonation and complex formation. Redox potential influences uranium and iron speciation. Engineers maintain strict control of aqueous chemistry, supported by continuous pH, conductivity, and redox monitoring.

Circuit modelling supports optimisation. Simulation tools predict distribution coefficients, loading curves, and stage requirements. Modelling identifies bottlenecks, predicts phase behaviour under upset conditions, and supports extractant selection. Models integrate temperature, acidity, impurity levels, and mass transfer coefficients. Scale up from laboratory to industrial circuits requires locked cycle tests, pilot plant trials, and dynamic modelling.

Solvent extraction remains central to rare earth separation because its chemical architecture allows fine tuning of interactions between trivalent cations and organic ligands. The method achieves high purity across the full lanthanide series with scalable performance and established industrial reliability.

Solvent extraction circuits require integrated control systems because separation of closely related lanthanides demands consistent mass transfer performance, stable phase composition, and finely tuned thermodynamic conditions. Operational stability depends on monitoring, automated adjustments, impurity management, and continuous solvent conditioning. Any deviation in acidity, temperature, extractant quality, or flow balance can degrade separation efficiency and reduce purity across the final product stream.

Process monitoring uses online sensors, laboratory assays, and automated sampling. pH probes track acidity gradients across extraction, scrubbing, and stripping banks. Conductivity sensors detect changes in ionic strength. Density meters verify phase composition. Optical devices monitor phase interface levels within settlers. Automated titration systems measure extractant degradation, total acid balance, and organic loading. Real time data informs control algorithms that adjust pump speed, reagent addition, and temperature. Control systems maintain phase continuity, prevent overloading, and stabilise equilibrium.

Organic phase stability requires continuous maintenance. Extractant degradation produces monoesters, phosphoric acid, and polymerised residues. These by products modify interfacial tension, reduce distribution coefficients, and promote third phase formation. Plants implement periodic carbon treatment to adsorb degradation residues. Filtration removes suspended solids introduced through upstream processes. Solvent regeneration units distil diluent to remove volatile impurities. Organic bleed streams remove a fraction of degraded solvent and maintain equilibrium composition. These measures maintain extraction performance across long campaigns.

Mixer settler design influences separation efficiency. Mixers use impellers to disperse one phase into another, forming droplets with controlled size distribution. Droplet size determines mass transfer surface area. Too small droplets increase entrainment and destabilise settlers. Too large droplets reduce mass transfer. Engineers control droplet size through impeller design, baffling, mixing energy, and phase ratio. Settlers require uniform flow distribution, controlled weir design, and minimised turbulence to enhance coalescence. Settler geometry influences phase separation. Wide, shallow settlers promote coalescence and reduce breakthrough of dispersed phase.

Solids management remains critical because fine particles enter solvent extraction circuits through incomplete filtration. Solids adsorb extractants, create nucleation sites for emulsions, and reduce settler performance. Filters must maintain clarity without excessive pressure drop. Filter failure introduces fines that destabilise the entire circuit. Plants install redundant filtration, online turbidity monitoring, and filter wash cycles to maintain performance.

Group separation requires careful design. Extraction circuits separate light rare earths (La–Nd), middle rare earths (Sm–Gd), and heavy rare earths (Tb–Lu, Y) into distinct streams. Engineers use extractant systems with distribution coefficients tailored to each group. Light rare earth circuits require weaker extractants and shorter banks. Heavy rare earth circuits require stronger extractants, higher acidity, and longer banks. Group separation efficiency influences the length of individual element circuits. Efficient group separation reduces the number of stages needed for refining downstream.

Individual element separation follows group separation. Each circuit isolates one rare earth from its neighbours based on distribution coefficient gradients. Adjacent elements show small differences, requiring many stages. Heavy rare earths require more stages because distribution coefficients converge. Engineers adjust acidity stepwise to enhance separation, increase scrub intensity, or add complexants to modify selectivity. High purity circuits require careful control of organic loading to prevent breakthrough of adjacent elements.

Temperature control influences distribution coefficients and viscosity. Cold conditions increase viscosity, reduce mass transfer, and slow phase disengagement. Hot conditions increase extractant degradation. Temperature control systems maintain optimal extraction conditions through heat exchangers, insulated piping, and continuous monitoring.

Waste treatment integrates with solvent extraction. Raffinate streams contain impurities removed during extraction. These streams require neutralisation, precipitation, or concentration before disposal. Organic phase wash solutions contain degraded extractant and dissolved metals. Wash solutions require treatment through carbon beds, chemical precipitation, or distillation. Proper waste management prevents contamination and ensures regulatory compliance.

Solvent extraction demands high operational discipline. Stability in flow, acidity, organic composition, and temperature determines purity. Integrated monitoring and control enable consistent separation of lanthanides at industrial scale. The technique remains essential because no alternative achieves comparable resolution across the entire rare earth series.

4.2 Ion exchange and membrane technologies

Ion exchange and membrane technologies provide alternative or complementary routes for separating rare earth elements from complex leach liquors. These methods exploit differences in ionic radius, charge density, hydration behaviour, and ligand affinity across the lanthanide series. They offer higher selectivity, reduced reagent consumption, and improved environmental performance in specific applications. Their main limitation remains lower throughput and higher cost compared with solvent extraction. They remain essential for high purity fractions, heavy rare earth isolation, and polishing steps where fine resolution outweighs volume requirements.

Ion exchange systems use solid phase resins with functional groups that bind rare earth ions through electrostatic attraction or coordination bonding. Cation exchange resins bearing sulfonic groups exchange protons for rare earth cations. Chelating resins bearing phosphonic, aminophosphonic, carboxylic, or iminodiacetic groups form inner sphere complexes with strong selectivity for particular lanthanides. Resin structure influences performance. Macroporous resins support fast mass transfer and resist fouling. Gel type resins provide high capacity but lower kinetics. Particle size influences loading rates and pressure drop. Engineers balance resin capacity, kinetic performance, and mechanical stability for each application.

Ion exchange follows adsorption and elution cycles. During adsorption, leach liquor flows through resin beds under controlled pH and ionic strength. Rare earths bind while impurities pass through or bind weakly. Uranium and thorium behaviour depends on oxidation state and resin functional group. During elution, reagents such as mineral acids, complexants, or chloride rich solutions release rare earths selectively. Elution gradients isolate groups or individual elements depending on resin selectivity and operating conditions. High resolution eluates undergo precipitation or crystallisation to obtain oxalates, carbonates, or chlorides.

Column design influences ion exchange efficiency. Fixed bed columns provide simple operation but suffer from channel formation and poor mass transfer at high flow. Expanded bed and fluidised bed columns improve mass transfer and reduce channeling. Packed bed columns require pretreatment to remove suspended solids that foul resin. Pretreatment includes filtration, pH adjustment, and removal of silica or iron. Resin regeneration cycles restore functional group activity but require management of waste streams containing concentrated impurities.

Membrane technologies provide separation through size exclusion, charge separation, or selective transport. Nanofiltration separates multivalent ions from monovalent ions through charged pores. Rare earth ions concentrate in the retentate while sodium, potassium, and other monovalent cations pass through. Nanofiltration reduces impurity load before solvent extraction or ion exchange. Reverse osmosis removes dissolved salts and concentrates rare earth solutions. These methods require high pressure pumps, scaling control, and antiscalants. Electrodialysis and electrodialysis with bipolar membranes exploit ion migration under electric fields. Bipolar membranes split water into hydrogen and hydroxyl ions, allowing pH gradients that separate rare earth ions from impurities. Electrodialysis targets separation of sulphate, chloride, or nitrate anions from rare earth cations. It reduces acid consumption in downstream solvent extraction. Membrane fouling by silica, iron hydroxides, and organic degradation products remains a major challenge. Engineers use pre filtration, antiscalants, and periodic backwashing to reduce fouling.

Supported liquid membranes integrate extractants within polymer membranes. Rare earth ions transfer across the membrane through liquid filled pores containing organophosphorus extractants. This method provides high selectivity with lower extractant inventory than solvent extraction. Its limitations include membrane stability, extractant leakage, and fouling. Hollow fibre supported membranes improve mass transfer through high surface area. Rare earth concentration and purity achievable through supported membranes suit polishing stages but not primary separation.

Ion exchange supports isolation of high purity heavy rare earths where solvent extraction becomes inefficient due to small distribution coefficient differences. Membrane systems support impurity removal, concentration, and pH control. Integrated systems may combine nanofiltration to concentrate feed, ion exchange to isolate groups, and supported membranes to refine purity. These hybrid flowsheets offer improved efficiency for small scale, high value applications.

Ion exchange and membrane technologies deliver high selectivity and precise control of rare earth separation in environments where solvent extraction alone proves insufficient. Their role grows in applications requiring environmental compliance, reduced organic solvent use, and production of ultra high purity products.

Ion exchange performance depends on resin chemistry, ligand strength, hydration energy, and transport kinetics. Rare earth ions display similar charge and only modest variation in ionic radius, so resin selectivity must exploit fine differences in ligand interaction. Chelating resins containing phosphonic or aminophosphonic groups remain most effective because these ligands form strong complexes with trivalent rare earth ions. Stability constants increase from light to heavy rare earths due to rising charge density and reduced hydration shell strength. Engineers exploit these trends through gradient elution. A stepwise increase in acidity, chloride concentration, or complexing agent strength elutes individual elements or groups.

Mass transfer in ion exchange occurs through film diffusion at the resin surface, pore diffusion within the resin, and chemical reaction at functional groups. Rate limiting steps depend on resin structure. Macroporous resins exhibit rapid film diffusion due to open pore networks. Gel type resins rely on slower pore diffusion. High ionic strength in leach liquors reduces activity coefficient of rare earth ions and slows adsorption. Engineers maintain appropriate flow rates, avoid channel formation, and manage resin bed expansion to preserve mass transfer rate. Column design uses distributors, flow straighteners, and residence time control to ensure uniform contact between resin and solution.

Resin fouling arises from iron hydroxides, aluminium hydroxides, silica, organic degradation products, and suspended solids. Fouling reduces resin capacity, blocks pores, and alters pH behaviour. Pretreatment removes fouling agents through filtration, clarification, oxidation, or pH adjustment. Iron removal may require controlled oxidation followed by precipitation. Silica requires pH control or magnesium induced coagulation. Organic foulants require activated carbon pre treatment. Resin cleaning cycles restore performance through acid or caustic washing.

Ion exchange regeneration requires careful management because regeneration waste streams contain concentrated impurities and radionuclides. Regeneration solutions must undergo neutralisation, precipitation, or ion exchange polishing before discharge or reuse. Resin mechanical integrity must withstand repeated regeneration cycles without fracture. Physical degradation increases fines, which migrate through columns and destabilise operation.

Membrane technologies require precise control of transmembrane pressure, cross flow velocity, and solution chemistry. Nanofiltration membranes permit passage of monovalent ions while retaining multivalent ions such as rare earths. Separation depends on membrane charge, pore size distribution, and hydration radius. High sulphate concentration increases osmotic pressure and reduces flux. Calcium and magnesium scale membranes through sulphate and carbonate precipitation. Antiscalants, pH adjustment, and controlled supersaturation reduce scaling. Cross flow velocity reduces cake layer formation. Periodic backwashing restores performance.

Reverse osmosis provides higher rejection but demands higher pressure. Rare earth solutions concentrated through reverse osmosis undergo reduced acid consumption in downstream processes. Membrane integrity depends on resistance to acids, chlorides, and oxidising species. Rare earth liquors often contain chloride, sulphate, and nitrate, which require membrane materials with chemical durability.

Electrodialysis depends on selective ion migration through cation and anion exchange membranes. Rare earth cations migrate under electric field but face competition from other multivalent ions. Membrane selectivity determines separation. Bipolar membranes split water to generate acid and base streams, allowing in situ pH adjustment. This reduces reliance on external chemicals. Electrodialysis reduces sulphate or chloride load in rare earth solutions, improving solvent extraction. Fouling arises from colloids, precipitates, and organic species. Cleaning cycles use acid or alkali fluids. Membrane stacking requires precise electrical control to avoid short circuiting or overheating.

Supported liquid membranes integrate extractants into polymer matrices. These systems replicate solvent extraction chemistry with lower solvent volume and higher surface area. Extractants dissolve in hydrophobic carriers immobilised in membrane pores. Rare earth ions transfer from feed into organic phase and then into strip solution. Efficiency depends on membrane stability, extractant retention, and mass transfer across thin films. Hollow fibre modules increase interfacial area. Challenges include extractant leakage, membrane wetting, chemical degradation, and fouling. These systems suit polishing operations and laboratory scale separations rather than bulk production.

Hybrid flowsheets integrate ion exchange and membrane technologies to overcome limitations of each method. Nanofiltration concentrates rare earth solutions and removes monovalent ions. Ion exchange isolates groups or high purity elements. Supported membranes refine final purity. Integration reduces organic solvent use and waste generation. These flowsheets require detailed modelling, pilot scale validation, and strict water chemistry control.

Ion exchange and membrane technologies offer precise control over separation chemistry in rare earth processing. They complement solvent extraction by providing high selectivity, reduced reagent consumption, and improved purity.

Ion exchange and membrane technologies require integrated chemical, mechanical, and operational control because rare earth solutions display complex behaviour driven by pH sensitivity, ionic strength, speciation, and impurity load. Stability across these systems determines separation efficiency, resin lifetime, membrane integrity, and product purity. Rare earth circuits that rely on these methods must manage fouling, scaling, competing ions, and variable feed chemistry with precision.

Ion exchange requires stable feed composition. Rare earth speciation changes rapidly with pH and ligand concentration. Light rare earths hydrolyse earlier than heavy rare earths. Hydrolysis produces polymeric species that adsorb poorly onto resin surfaces. Engineers maintain narrow pH windows to preserve trivalent ionic form. Oxidation state influences uranium behaviour. UV^{6+} binds strongly to certain resins but interferes with rare earth loading. Reducing agents convert UV^{6+} to U^{4+}, reducing competition. Thorium forms strong hydrolysed species that interact with resin functional groups at low pH. Dedicated thorium removal steps prevent resin overload.

Column hydrodynamics influence adsorption. Velocity must remain within limits to prevent fluidisation of resin beads while ensuring adequate mass transfer. Maldistribution of flow creates channeling, reducing utilisation of resin capacity. Engineers design distributors to create uniform flow. Backwashing expands resin bed to remove fines, redistribute beads, and restore bed porosity. Excessive backwashing fractures beads and reduces capacity. Fines production clogs downstream filters and destabilises operation.

Elution requires controlled gradients. Acid elution must avoid excessive proton concentration that strips multiple elements simultaneously. Chelating elution uses ligands such as EDTA derivatives that preferentially complex specific rare earths. Chloride elution exploits differences in chloride complex stability. Engineers design multi step gradients to release rare earths selectively. Gradient design must account for resin capacity, diffusion rate, and competitive binding.

Membrane technologies require control of scaling, fouling, and chemical stability. Nanofiltration membranes experience scaling from calcium sulphate, calcium carbonate, silica, and rare earth precipitates. Scale inhibitors reduce nucleation. pH control limits supersaturation. Feed softening removes calcium and magnesium. Silica control requires careful pH adjustment or magnesium induced stabilisation. Organic fouling arises from humic acids, degradation products, or organophosphorus residues. Pre filtration, activated carbon, and coagulation reduce foulants. Membrane cleaning uses acid, caustic, or enzymatic solutions. Cleaning frequency influences membrane life and operational cost.

Electrodialysis performance depends on membrane selectivity, electrical resistance, and fouling control. Rare earth ions migrate slowly compared with monovalent ions. Competitive migration reduces selectivity. Bipolar membranes require stable electric field and controlled temperature. Overheating degrades membrane structure. Scaling in electrodialysis stacks increases resistance and reduces current efficiency. Stack design requires flow distributors, turbulence promoters, and controlled pressure.

Supported liquid membranes require extractant retention, chemical compatibility, and membrane integrity. Extractant leaching reduces performance and contaminates product. Membrane wetting reduces selectivity and accelerates degradation. Engineers select polymer matrices with appropriate pore size, hydrophobicity, and mechanical strength. Operating conditions must remain within limits to prevent phase breakthrough. Long term stability remains a challenge.

Hybrid systems integrate multiple technologies to overcome individual limitations. Rare earth solutions may pass through nanofiltration to remove monovalent ions and reduce impurity load. Ion exchange isolates heavy rare earths with high resolution. Supported membranes perform final polishing. Hybrid flowsheets require complete understanding of feed chemistry, resin behaviour, membrane fouling, and mass transfer. Modelling tools simulate performance under variable composition, temperature, and flow. Pilot studies validate flowsheets before industrial deployment.

Ion exchange and membrane technologies serve as critical tools where solvent extraction lacks selectivity, where environmental regulations restrict organic solvent use, or where ultra high purity elements are required. Their integration into rare earth refining enhances flexibility, reduces waste, and improves control across high value product streams.

4.3 Metal production and alloy fabrication

Metal production and alloy fabrication convert refined rare earth compounds into metallic lanthanides and engineered alloys used in magnets, hydrogen storage systems, aerospace components, and advanced electronics. Rare earth metals require specialised reduction routes because their high reactivity, low electronegativity, and affinity for oxygen, nitrogen, and hydrogen prevent direct smelting. Their production demands controlled atmospheres, high purity reagents, and precise thermodynamic management. Each rare earth displays unique reduction behaviour that dictates reactor design, flux composition, and purification method.

The primary industrial route uses metallothermic reduction of anhydrous rare earth chlorides. Chlorides arise from conversion of rare earth oxides through high temperature chlorination using carbon tetrachloride, ammonium chloride, or chlorine gas mixed with carbon. Chlorination requires inert atmosphere to prevent oxychloride formation. Conversion efficiency depends on temperature, residence time, and chloride partial pressure. Resulting anhydrous chlorides feed metallothermic reactors where calcium, lithium, or magnesium reductants capture chlorine to form stable halides. Reduction occurs in sealed refractory lined vessels under inert gas. Heat balance remains critical because reduction initiates exothermic reactions that risk runaway if not moderated. Calcium based systems dominate because $CaCl_2$ displays stable behaviour and high melting point.

Metal forms as a molten phase beneath the salt flux. Separation requires density contrast between metal and salt. Rare earth metals exhibit high density relative to $CaCl_2$ flux, allowing gravity separation. Flux viscosity and surface tension influence coalescence of metal droplets. Engineers adjust flux composition through $CaCl_2$–CaF_2 mixtures to control melting point and viscosity. After cooling, salt blocks break mechanically to extract metal ingots. Residual salt removal requires thermal treatment or vacuum distillation.

Vacuum distillation purifies rare earth metals after reduction. Each metal displays distinct vapour pressure behaviour. Light rare earths such as lanthanum, cerium, and praseodymium volatilise more readily than heavy rare earths. Distillation occurs under high vacuum and controlled temperature gradients. Impurities such as Ca, Mg, Cl, O, N, and H migrate into vapour phase or residual slag depending on thermodynamic stability. Condensation surfaces collect purified rare earth metal films. Engineers design distillation columns with high surface area, controlled thermal zones, and inert gas purging to prevent oxidation. Distillation produces high purity metals suitable for alloying and advanced applications.

Electrolytic reduction provides another route for specific rare earths. Molten salt electrolysis uses rare earth chlorides dissolved in eutectic salt mixtures. Electrolysis requires oxygen free atmospheres and corrosion resistant electrodes. Cathodic deposition forms metallic lanthanides, while anodic reactions evolve chlorine gas. Electrolytic cells require strict temperature control because rare earth chlorides decompose or volatilise if overheated. Electrolysis suits rare earths where metallothermic reduction proves inefficient due to complex impurity profiles or low reduction potential.

Alloy fabrication requires precise control of composition, melting behaviour, and cooling rate. Rare earth alloys include NdFeB, SmCo, mischmetal based alloys, hydrogen storage alloys, and high temperature aerospace materials. NdFeB magnet alloys form through controlled melting of neodymium, iron, and boron in vacuum induction furnaces. Oxygen content must remain extremely low because Nd oxidises readily. Alloy melt requires inert gas cover or ultra high vacuum. Rapid solidification improves magnetic performance by refining grain size and preventing formation of undesirable phases. Strip casting produces thin flakes that undergo hydrogen decrepitation, milling, pressing, and sintering to create high performance magnets.

SmCo alloys require higher melting temperatures, controlled cobalt ratios, and slow cooling to stabilise the $SmCo_5$ or Sm_2Co_{17} phases. These alloys offer superior high temperature stability. Production requires vacuum arc melting or induction melting with ceramic or refractory lined crucibles resistant to cobalt attack. Heat treatment after casting adjusts microstructure and enhances magnetic properties.

Mischmetal alloys, composed primarily of lanthanum, cerium, neodymium, and praseodymium, support lighter industrial uses. Mischmetal reacts with iron, nickel, and silicon to create flints, hydrogen storage alloys, and deoxidisers. Hydrogen storage alloys require controlled activation to create interstitial hydrogen sites. Alloying introduces elements such as Mg, Ni, Co, Mn, and Al to stabilise hydride formation. Production requires inert atmospheres, controlled cooling, and hydrogen conditioning.

Metallic purity influences alloy behaviour. Trace oxygen increases brittleness. Nitrogen embrittles heavy rare earth metals. Carbon and sulphur alter phase stability. Chlorine residues form inclusions. Purity control requires vacuum induction melting, degassing, and filtration. Casting technology influences grain structure. Chill casting creates fine structures. Vacuum moulding reduces oxidation. Powder metallurgy supports uniform phase distribution and minimises segregation.

Rare earth metal production and alloy fabrication require integration of thermodynamics, metallurgy, materials engineering, and environmental control. High reactivity, contamination risk, and narrow specification windows demand sophisticated equipment and strict operational discipline.

Metal production performance depends on controlled thermodynamic pathways, reagent purity, and containment of reactive intermediates. Rare earth metals form through reduction of oxides, fluorides, or chlorides. Each reduction route demands precise temperature control, phase stability, and inert conditions because rare earths oxidise, nitridise, and hydride rapidly. Engineers choose reduction pathways based on feed composition, impurity profile, cost, and desired metal purity.

Oxide reduction through metallothermic pathways requires conversion of oxides to halides because direct reduction of rare earth oxides with carbon or hydrogen produces carbides, hydrides, or mixed compounds unsuitable for alloying. Chlorination converts oxides into stable chlorides. Chlorination systems include rotary kilns, fluidised beds, or static reactors. Fluidised beds provide uniform heat distribution and continuous chlorination. Chlorination removes fluorine, carbonate, and water. Product quality depends on dryness, particle size, and absence of oxychlorides. Anhydrous chlorides feed metallothermic reactors where calcium or lithium reductants drive reduction. Reaction by products include $CaCl_2$ or $LiCl$ fluxes. Flux composition influences melting point and density. Engineers adjust flux composition to maximise metal separation.

Thermodynamic modelling supports reduction design. Gibbs free energy calculations identify optimal temperature for reduction. Calcium reduces rare earth chlorides efficiently because $CaCl_2$ has strong thermodynamic stability. Lithium reduces specific rare earths when low melting fluxes required. Magnesium reduction occurs at higher temperatures and produces $MgCl_2$ flux with different fluidity. Reaction kinetics depend on particle size, mixing, and contact surface. Engineers design batch or semi continuous reactors with stirring mechanisms that allow efficient contact between flux and chloride feed. Reaction products cool in controlled steps to avoid metal oxidation.

Vacuum systems support metal purification. Rare earth metals contain dissolved gases, residual halides, and metallic impurities after reduction. Vacuum distillation removes volatile halides such as $CaCl_2$, $MgCl_2$, and LiCl. Distillation requires multi zone furnaces with controlled temperature gradients, radiant heating, and vacuum pumps. Vapour pressure varies across rare earths. Light rare earths volatilise at lower temperatures, requiring precise control to avoid loss. Distillation yields high purity metals with low oxygen, nitrogen, hydrogen, and halogen content.

Electrolytic reduction supports production of specific rare earths at high purity. Molten salt electrolysis dissolves rare earth chlorides in eutectic mixtures of NaCl, KCl, or $CaCl_2$. Cathode design influences deposition morphology. Deposition occurs as fine dendritic structures that require melting to form ingots. Anode gas evolution produces chlorine, requiring robust scrubbing. Cell design prevents rare earth metal contamination from anode materials. Electrolytic reduction achieves high purity with controlled conditions but remains energy intensive. Electrolyte management demands periodic removal of accumulated impurities.

Alloy fabrication integrates rare earth metals with transition metals, refractory metals, or light metals. NdFeB magnet alloys require precise control of neodymium content. Excess neodymium improves coercivity but reduces mechanical strength. Alloy melting occurs in vacuum induction furnaces. Melting under inert gas prevents oxidation. Alloy homogenisation ensures uniform distribution of $Nd_2Fe_{14}B$ phase. Rapid solidification through strip casting forms thin flakes with refined microstructure. Hydrogen decrepitation fractures flakes into fine powder. Jet milling produces narrow particle size distribution. Pressing and sintering align grains and produce final magnets with strong anisotropy.

SmCo alloys require different microstructural control. $SmCo_5$ and Sm_2Co_{17} phases require controlled cooling to stabilise correct stoichiometry. Excess cobalt stabilises high temperature phases. Alloy melting demands precise temperature management to avoid Sm loss through evaporation. Vacuum arc melting maintains stoichiometry by reducing volatilisation. Heat treatment alters domain wall behaviour and improves magnetic performance.

Hydrogen storage alloys require formation of intermetallic compounds with controlled lattice parameters. Mischmetal Mg Ni Co Mn alloys require activation through hydrogen cycling to create pathways for hydrogen diffusion. Alloy brittleness supports activation but reduces mechanical strength. Fabrication requires controlled casting, annealing, and surface modification to improve hydrogen kinetics.

Aerospace alloys use rare earth additions such as yttrium, scandium, and mischmetal to improve grain refinement, oxidation resistance, and high temperature performance. Rare earth additions modify oxide dispersion and grain boundary behaviour. Alloy melting requires vacuum induction or electron beam melting to ensure purity. Microstructure control influences creep resistance and fatigue behaviour.

Quality control requires chemical analysis, microstructural characterisation, and mechanical testing. Spectroscopy identifies trace impurities. Metallography examines grain structure. Thermal analysis reveals phase transitions. Magnetic testing verifies coercivity and remanence in magnet alloys. Hydrogen absorption testing validates storage capacity. Casting defects, inclusions, or segregation undermine performance and require correction.

Rare earth metal and alloy production integrates reduction, melting, purification, and thermo mechanical processing. These processes create high performance materials essential for advanced technologies.

Metal production and alloy fabrication require integration of thermochemical control, furnace engineering, purification strategy, and microstructure design. Rare earth metals remain challenging due to their extreme reactivity, narrow tolerance for impurities, and sensitivity to oxygen, nitrogen, hydrogen, and residual halides. Each step from reduction to alloying depends on maintaining inert atmospheres, precise thermal gradients, and controlled kinetics to avoid unwanted phases.

Process control begins during chloride preparation. Anhydrous chloride production requires complete removal of water because hydrated chlorides decompose or hydrolyse during reduction, forming oxides and oxychlorides that trap rare earths. Water content below a few hundred ppm remains essential. Engineers use multi stage drying systems that combine rotary drying, vacuum drying, and chemical drying under inert gas. Feedstock purity determines reduction yield. Impurity elements such as iron, aluminium, and silicon influence reduction kinetics and alloy behaviour. Analytical control uses ICP OES, XRF, and gas analysers to measure impurities continuously.

During metallothermic reduction, reactor design influences product purity and safety. Furnaces require refractory linings resistant to halides and reducing agents. Furnace geometry influences heat distribution, reaction kinetics, and gas flow. Engineers design reactors to minimise dead zones where incomplete reduction occurs. Calcium reductant purity affects reaction kinetics. Residual oxygen or moisture in reductant produces CaO, reducing effective reduction capacity. Flux chemistry determines melting point, viscosity, and density. $CaCl_2$ based flux systems require strict control of chloride ratio because deviations influence rare earth metal coalescence. Flux circulation patterns influence droplet growth, metal coalescence, and final ingot morphology.

Metal refining requires hydride formation control. Rare earth metals absorb hydrogen readily, forming brittle hydrides. Hydrogen ingress occurs during cooling or handling. Vacuum annealing removes hydrogen and restores ductility. Nitrogen embrittlement occurs when metals contact nitrogen at high temperature. Nitride formation reduces mechanical strength and magnetic performance. Oxygen contamination produces rare earth oxides that create inclusions and disrupt microstructure. These impurities require removal through vacuum refining and inert atmosphere handling.

Alloy melting demands crucible materials compatible with rare earth reactivity. Zirconia, yttria stabilised crucibles, and high purity graphite resist attack. Crucible contamination introduces unwanted elements into alloy. Alloy melting requires multi step deoxidation using rare earth metals themselves or zirconium additions. Vacuum induction furnaces provide controlled melting with electromagnetic stirring that homogenises alloy composition. Temperature control avoids overheating, which increases volatilisation of light rare earths. Casting occurs under vacuum or inert gas. Solidification rate influences grain size and phase distribution. Rapid solidification produces fine grains and desirable magnetic or mechanical properties.

Powder metallurgy dominates high performance magnet fabrication. NdFeB powders require controlled particle size distribution, shape, and surface chemistry. Hydrogen decrepitation fractures cast alloys. Jet milling reduces particle size while avoiding oxidation. Powder mixing requires inert gas to avoid oxygen uptake. Magnetic alignment occurs during pressing. Sintering requires controlled temperature and atmosphere to avoid neodymium oxidation. Grain boundary diffusion processes introduce heavy rare earths such as dysprosium or terbium to increase coercivity. Diffusion requires precise temperature and time control to distribute elements along grain boundaries without excessive penetration that reduces magnetisation.

SmCo powders require different processing because SmCo alloys crystallise into distinct phases. Alloy melting requires tight control of stoichiometry because Sm loss through volatilisation alters phase balance. Milling breaks down brittle intermetallics. Powder pressing and sintering require high temperature under inert conditions. Heat treatment stabilises domains and enhances coercivity.

Alloys for hydrogen storage require microstructures that permit rapid hydrogen diffusion. Mischmetal based AB_5 alloys require annealing to create controlled grain boundary paths. Additives such as cobalt and manganese alter plateau pressure and capacity. Alloy surfaces require activation through repeated hydrogen cycling to improve kinetics. Microstructural stability determines long term hydrogen absorption performance.

Aerospace and structural alloys use rare earth additions to improve creep resistance, oxidation behaviour, and grain boundary stability. Yttrium and scandium refine grains and stabilise oxide films. Alloy melting requires electron beam furnaces or vacuum induction units to avoid contamination. Heat treatment produces controlled precipitates that improve high temperature performance.

Quality assurance remains essential. Analytical chemistry ensures purity. Metallography confirms phase distribution. Mechanical testing validates strength, toughness, and fatigue performance. Magnetic testing measures coercivity, remanence, and energy product. Any deviation in purity or microstructure undermines performance.

Rare earth metal production and alloy fabrication demand integrated process engineering that respects the extreme reactivity and narrow processing windows of these elements. The resulting metals and alloys support critical technologies across energy, transport, defence, and electronics.

4.4 Recycling pathways

Recycling pathways recover rare earths from end of life products, industrial scrap, and process residues. These pathways reduce primary mining demand, stabilise supply chains, and reduce waste. Rare earth recycling remains complex because these elements occur in small quantities, dispersed across devices, embedded in alloys, bonded in magnets, or locked within phosphors. Effective recovery requires controlled dismantling, selective liberation, targeted separation, and re processing through hydrometallurgical or pyrometallurgical routes. Each feed category requires its own technical pathway because chemical form, impurity load, and physical structure differ across applications.

Permanent magnets represent the most attractive recycling feedstock due to high concentrations of neodymium, praseodymium, dysprosium, and terbium. Magnet waste arises from end of life motors, hard disk drives, wind turbines, industrial machinery, and manufacturing scrap. Magnets often exist as sintered NdFeB blocks embedded in housings, resin bonded structures, or epoxy coated components. Recovery begins with mechanical dismantling. Manual or robotic disassembly identifies magnets, removes housings, and isolates magnet assemblies. Magnets require demagnetisation through thermal treatment or alternating magnetic fields. Thermal demagnetisation occurs at two hundred to four hundred degrees Celsius, lowering coercivity and allowing safe handling.

Mechanical processing follows demagnetisation. Shredding, crushing, and milling liberate magnet fragments. Hydrogen decrepitation provides an alternative route. Exposure to hydrogen fractures NdFeB magnets due to hydride formation, producing fine powder with preserved composition. Hydrogen decrepitation reduces energy use and improves selectivity. Powder purification removes coatings, adhesives, and metallic contaminants. Magnetic separation removes steel, copper, and aluminium. Sieving ensures narrow particle size distribution.

Hydrometallurgical recycling dissolves magnet powder in acid. Hydrochloric or sulphuric acid leaching converts rare earths into salts while dissolving iron and boron. Selective precipitation removes iron through pH control or oxidation. Rare earths remain in solution due to lower hydrolysis tendency. Solvent extraction separates neodymium, praseodymium, and dysprosium. Stripping produces rare earth chloride or nitrate solutions. Oxalate precipitation then yields pure rare earth oxalates, which calcine to oxides. These oxides feed metal reduction and magnet fabrication routes. Hydrometallurgical recycling requires impurity control because coatings and lubricants introduce organics, aluminium, and silicon.

Pyrometallurgical recycling bypasses dissolution. Smelting in controlled atmospheres reduces iron, producing rare earth rich slag. Rare earth oxides concentrate in slag, which then undergoes halide conversion and metallothermic reduction. Carbothermic routes reduce iron but must avoid carbide formation that traps rare earths. Vacuum arc furnaces melt scrap magnets, producing alloy ingots with controlled composition. These ingots require refinement to remove carbon, oxygen, and nitrogen. Pyrometallurgical recycling suits bulk magnet waste streams but requires high energy input.

Battery recycling provides another rare earth source, especially from nickel metal hydride (NiMH) batteries used in hybrid vehicles. NiMH batteries contain mischmetal alloys rich in lanthanum, cerium, neodymium, and praseodymium. Recycling begins with mechanical dismantling and separation of battery electrodes. Hydride forming alloys dissolve in acid, releasing rare earths. Nickel and cobalt separate through solvent extraction or precipitation. Rare earths precipitate as oxalates or carbonates. Calcination yields rare earth oxides. Process complexity depends on electrode design, binder composition, and impurity load from battery casings.

Phosphor recycling targets europium, terbium, and yttrium in fluorescent lamps, LEDs, and display panels. Phosphors occur as thin coatings containing red (Y_2O_3:Eu), green ($LaPO_4$:Ce,Tb), and blue ($BaMgAl_{10}O_{17}$:Eu) materials. Recycling begins with lamp crushing in controlled systems to capture mercury. Phosphor powder separates through air classification or wet separation. Acid leaching dissolves rare earths. Insoluble matrix materials require thermal treatment or alkali fusion to improve leachability. Rare earths separate through solvent extraction. Purification requires removal of aluminium, barium, strontium, and arsenic impurities. Phosphor recycling delivers high purity rare earths but remains constrained by low collection rates.

Catalyst recycling targets cerium in automotive catalysts and fluid catalytic cracking units. Cerium exists as ceria coatings on supports such as alumina or zeolite. Mechanical recovery yields spent catalyst powder. Acid leaching dissolves cerium, but support materials remain. Cerium precipitates as hydroxide or oxalate. Catalyst recycling remains economically viable only when large volumes accumulate. Impurity management remains complex due to hydrocarbons, heavy metals, and sulphuraceous deposits.

Recycling from industrial residues includes slag, leach residues, and process dust containing rare earths. Carbonatite operations produce low grade residues with recoverable rare earths. Red mud from bauxite refining contains rare earths in low concentrations. Processing requires aggressive leaching or pyrometallurgical concentration. These pathways remain emerging due to low grade and complex impurity profiles.

Recycling pathways require integration with product design. Designing magnets, batteries, catalysts, and phosphors for disassembly increases yield. Avoiding coatings and adhesives improves processing efficiency.

Labelling components with material composition supports automated sorting. These design changes enhance circularity and reduce reliance on primary mining.

Rare earth recycling requires coordinated dismantling, liberation, and separation technologies. Major pathways include magnet recycling, battery recycling, phosphor recycling, catalyst recovery, and industrial residue processing. Each pathway requires precise metallurgical control to yield high purity rare earths suitable for re entry into advanced manufacturing.

Recycling pathways depend on controlled material flows, precise separation chemistry, and tailored processing routes for each product type. Rare earth bearing wastes vary in physical structure, chemical composition, and impurity burden, forcing each recycling line to adopt its own liberation and refining logic. High purity outputs require strict management of contaminants originating from coatings, binders, lubricants, casings, plastics, ceramics, and metal alloys associated with end of life devices.

Permanent magnet recycling presents several parallel routes. Direct reuse recycles magnets without breaking them down into rare earth oxides or metals. Direct reuse retains magnetic phases but restores performance through powder processing. Hydrogen decrepitation converts sintered NdFeB magnets into powders that retain $Nd_2Fe_{14}B$ structure with controlled grain boundary phases. These powders undergo jet milling, pressing, and sintering to recreate new magnets. Direct reuse avoids complex separation steps and reduces energy consumption. However, magnet composition varies across applications, creating inconsistency and restricting direct reuse to magnet scraps with known composition.

Indirect hydrometallurgical recycling dissolves magnets fully. Leaching systems require controlled ratios of acid to metal to avoid excessive dissolution of iron and boron. Engineers use selective precipitation to remove iron before rare earth separation. Iron removal may involve oxidation followed by hydrolysis or complexation with organic ligands. Rare earth solutions then undergo solvent extraction using organophosphorus extractants. Multi stage extraction isolates Nd, Pr, Dy, and Tb. Oxalate precipitation yields mixed or individual oxalates. Calcination produces rare earth oxides suitable for metallothermic reduction. Hydrometallurgical recycling achieves high purity but generates acid residues that require neutralisation.

Pyrometallurgical recycling suits magnet scrap with coatings, impurities, or variable composition. Smelting under reducing atmosphere produces iron rich metal and rare earth rich slag. Rare earth oxidation during smelting yields stable oxides that partition into slag. Subsequent chloride or fluoride conversion dissolves rare earth oxides for reduction or solvent extraction. Slag must maintain controlled basicity, viscosity, and phase structure to ensure rare earth partitioning. Engineers control furnace temperature, slag chemistry, and reduction potential to preserve rare earth yield.

Battery recycling from NiMH units requires material separation at electrode level. Mechanical shredding liberates hydride alloy particles from nickel foils. Magnetic separation removes steel casings. Alkali washing removes potassium hydroxide electrolyte. Alloy dissolution requires acid leaching under controlled oxidation state because hydride alloys contain multiple metallic phases. Nickel and cobalt separate through solvent extraction or precipitation. Rare earths precipitate as carbonates or oxalates. Battery recycling purity depends on electrode contamination, ageing effects, and binder residues.

Phosphor recycling focuses on light sources containing europium, terbium, and yttrium. Phosphors adhere to glass tubes through binders. Recovery requires crushing and air classification under mercury controlled conditions. Mercury removal precedes phosphor treatment. Phosphor fractions contain mixtures of red, green, and blue phosphors. Density separation and selective leaching isolate individual fractions. Red phosphors dissolve in acids more readily than green or blue. Green phosphors require stronger acids or oxidative treatments. Blue phosphors resist dissolution and require fusion or thermal activation. Rare earth solutions undergo solvent extraction or ion exchange. Phosphor recycling yields high purity but remains limited by decreasing use of fluorescent lamps.

Catalyst recycling processes large volumes of spent FCC and automotive catalysts. Cerium in FCC catalysts exists as dispersed ceria particles. Mechanical treatment liberates catalyst fines. Acid leaching dissolves cerium while leaving alumina support. Hydrothermal treatments enhance cerium mobility. Cerium purification requires precipitation or solvent extraction. Automotive catalysts contain ceria zirconia mixtures, platinum group metals, and complex supports. Rare earth recovery focuses mainly on cerium. Recovery economics depend on catalyst composition and platinum group metals.

Industrial residue recycling targets slag, red mud, and process residues. Red mud contains rare earths but requires aggressive leaching due to low grade and complex mineralogy. Acid leaching dissolves rare earths but mobilises iron, aluminium, and titanium. Selective precipitation or solvent extraction removes these impurities. Carbonatite residues contain secondary rare earth phases that dissolve under mild acid. Process residues require characterisation, mineralogical analysis, and tailored leaching conditions.

Recycling pathways perform optimally under closed loop systems. Closed loop magnet recycling returns rare earths directly to magnet fabrication with minimal purity degradation. Closed loop phosphor recycling recovers europium and terbium for new phosphors. Closed loop battery recycling reintroduces lanthanum and cerium into hydride alloys. Closed loop systems reduce contamination, improve recovery, and stabilise material quality.

Recycling remains constrained by collection, sorting, and feed availability. Mixed waste streams reduce purity and complicate processing. Design for recycling improves performance by reducing adhesives, coatings, and composite layers. Standardised housings and material labels support robotic disassembly. Wider adoption of these practices enhances circularity.

Rare earth recycling requires targeted liberation, selective separation, and controlled chemical processing. High value pathways such as magnet and phosphor recycling remain the most advanced, while battery and residue recycling continue to expand with improved technologies.

Recycling pathways require integration of dismantling technology, material identification, chemical separation, and re manufacturing. Each pathway must overcome physical, chemical, logistical, and regulatory constraints because rare earth-bearing devices are diverse, geographically dispersed, and often embedded within composite structures. The technical efficiency of recycling depends on enabling technologies that streamline feed preparation, optimise reaction conditions, and maintain purity across the final product stream.

Feed preparation influences recovery more than any downstream step. Accurate identification of rare earth-containing components remains essential. Manual dismantling remains reliable but labour intensive. Automated approaches use machine vision, spectroscopy, and robotics to identify magnets, batteries, and phosphor modules. Laser induced breakdown spectroscopy identifies rare earth signatures in embedded components. X ray fluorescence detects neodymium in motor assemblies or europium in phosphors. Automated dismantling reduces contamination from plastics, adhesives, and coatings.

Liberation follows identification. Mechanical liberation includes shredding, crushing, milling, and magnetic separation. Liberation must balance particle size reduction with contamination risk. Over crushing embeds coatings and metals into powders, reducing leaching efficiency. Under crushing reduces liberation. Engineers optimise liberation parameters through real time particle analysis and magnetic extraction. Thermal liberation removes adhesives, binders, and polymers. Controlled pyrolysis decomposes organics without oxidising rare earth components. Laser ablation offers selective removal of coatings from magnets, improving hydrometallurgical efficiency.

Chemical recycling demands strict control of leaching conditions. Leaching efficiency depends on acid concentration, redox potential, solid to liquid ratio, and temperature. Rare earth magnets require leaching conditions that dissolve rare earth phases selectively while limiting iron dissolution. Additives complex iron, reducing interference. Battery alloys require oxidative conditions to dissolve multimetal hydrides. Phosphors require selective dissolution conditions because mixed phosphors respond differently to acid strength and oxidising species. Recycling processes require staged leaching where more reactive components dissolve first, reducing impurity load in later stages.

Separation relies on solvent extraction, ion exchange, or precipitation. Solvent extraction isolates neodymium, praseodymium, dysprosium, and terbium from magnet leachates. Distribution coefficients shift due to high iron and boron concentrations, requiring modified extractant systems. Ion exchange isolates europium and terbium in phosphor recycling due to their distinct ligand affinity. Precipitation yields oxalates or carbonates. Precipitation behaviour depends on pH, supersaturation, and impurities. Engineers design agitation, seeding, and temperature conditions to control particle size and morphology. Post precipitation washing removes soluble impurities.

Thermal processing converts precipitates to oxides. Calcination temperature determines oxide phase purity, surface area, and reactivity. High calcination temperatures increase crystallinity but reduce surface area, affecting reduction behaviour. Oxide purity influences metal reduction. Trace impurities such as Si, Al, Fe, and P reduce reduction efficiency and alloy performance. Process control maintains oxide purity within narrow limits.

Pyrometallurgical recycling requires furnace technologies designed for heterogeneous feed. Plasma furnaces produce high temperatures and allow rapid decomposition of organics and alloys. Induction furnaces melt magnet scrap with controlled atmosphere. Slag engineering separates rare earth oxides from metallic phases. Slag must maintain appropriate basicity to dissolve rare earth oxides. Engineers adjust flux composition and furnace temperature to stabilise slag behaviour. Off gas systems capture volatiles and particulates.

Closed loop recycling depends on re entry of recycled rare earths into magnet, battery, or phosphor production. Closed loop magnets require consistent Nd Pr Dy Tb ratios. Deviations degrade magnetic performance. Closed loop phosphors require europium and terbium purity above industry thresholds. Closed loop batteries require controlled mischmetal composition. These constraints force recycling processes to maintain narrow composition tolerances and prevent cross contamination.

Regulatory factors influence recycling. Collection systems determine feed availability. Hazardous waste regulations govern handling of mercury containing lamps, battery casings, and contaminated materials. Transport regulations apply to magnet scrap due to potential magnetic interference. Facilities require environmental controls for dust, acids, alkalis, and heavy metals. Compliance increases cost but remains necessary.

Economic viability depends on feed quality, process efficiency, purity requirements, and market demand. High value pathways such as NdFeB magnet recycling remain attractive. Lower value pathways such as red mud or low grade catalyst recycling require improved technology or co recovery of multiple metals. Emerging approaches include bioleaching, mechanochemical activation, and ionic liquid leaching. Bioleaching uses microbes to mobilise rare earths from phosphors and ores. Mechanochemical activation enhances leachability through high energy milling. Ionic liquids dissolve rare earth oxides selectively but require solvent stability and recovery systems.

Recycling pathways form a critical component of supply security. They rely on advanced dismantling, precise chemical separation, and re manufacturing technologies. Their development remains essential for high value applications and long term resource sustainability.

4.5 Technological barriers in high-purity refinement
High purity refinement of rare earth elements faces structural, chemical, and operational barriers rooted in the intrinsic similarity of lanthanide ions, their sensitivity to trace impurities, and the complex behaviour of intermediate species formed during separation. Purity thresholds for advanced technologies often exceed 99.99 percent and, for laser crystals, phosphors, and high performance magnets, rise above 99.999 percent. Attaining these levels requires precise control of

thermodynamic equilibria, kinetic pathways, solvent systems, redox stability, and impurity transport mechanisms. Each refinement stage introduces opportunities for contamination, loss of resolution, or instability in complex formation. These barriers impose limits on throughput, energy efficiency, and scalability.

The first barrier arises from the narrow chemical differences across the lanthanide series. Ionic radii shrink gradually from lanthanum to lutetium. Hydration enthalpies follow the same trend. Complex stability with ligands displays only modest deviation across neighbouring elements. Separation relies on small differences in distribution coefficients or stability constants. These differences shrink for heavy rare earths, making it difficult to separate them without large extraction banks, steep acidity gradients, or multiple re extraction cycles. Any deviation in pH, ionic strength, or extractant composition reduces resolution and introduces cross contamination. Heavy rare earth circuits require extended mixer settler chains or ion exchange columns with long bed depths. These increase operational cost and reduce throughput.

A second barrier arises from impurity behaviour. Trace elements such as iron, aluminium, titanium, thorium, and uranium form complexes that follow rare earths through solvent extraction or ion exchange. Even sub ppm levels of iron alter colour, magnetic behaviour, optical absorption, and mechanical properties of final products. Thorium and uranium introduce radiological constraints. Removal of these impurities requires additional scrub stages, complexants, and tight pH control. Impurities adsorb onto equipment surfaces and re contaminate product streams during stripping. Extractant degradation products mimic ligand behaviour, trapping metals or changing interfacial tension. These residues form stable emulsions and third phases that degrade separation. Purification demands regular solvent regeneration and bleed streams that reduce circuit stability.

A third barrier originates from the instability of intermediate species. Rare earths form multiple complexes depending on pH, ligand concentration, counter ions, and redox environment. Hydrolysed species precipitate prematurely and trap impurities. Chloride complexes behave differently from nitrate or sulphate complexes. Minor drift in acid concentration shifts equilibrium, altering distribution coefficients by measurable margins. Heavy rare earth complexes stabilise differently in solvent systems containing phosphonic or phosphinic acids. Temperature variation changes viscosity, diffusivity, and ligand protonation. These sensitivities force operators to maintain narrow control windows through automated dosing, inline monitoring, and model predictive control. Any departure from steady state multiplies error in purity.

A fourth barrier arises from equipment limitations. Mixer settlers require stable phase continuity and rapid phase disengagement. Fouling, entrainment, and solids contamination reduce efficiency. Ion exchange columns require uniform flow distribution; channel formation or resin swelling reduces theoretical plates. Membrane systems require precise pore integrity and chemical stability. Membrane wetting, fouling, or degradation collapses selectivity. Vacuum distillation requires high thermal uniformity and strong refractory stability. Minor leaks introduce oxygen, forming oxides or nitrides that reduce purity. Electrode degradation in electrolysis introduces metallic impurities that migrate into product. Equipment lifespan shortens in corrosive solvent systems, increasing maintenance burden.

A fifth barrier arises from thermodynamic constraints during final purification. At ultra high purity levels, removal of elements with similar vapour pressures, lattice radii, or chemical affinities becomes difficult. Vacuum distillation purifies light rare earths only when vapour pressure differences remain large. Heavy rare earths display close vapour pressures, limiting distillation. Zone refining improves purity for metals with directional solidification behaviour, but rare earth metal reactivity complicates zone stability. Solid state diffusion purifies some alloys, but kinetics remain slow due to complex phase diagrams. These limits restrict the choice of purification technologies.

High purity products require rigorous contamination control. Water, oxygen, nitrogen, carbon, sulphur, chlorine, and fluorine each degrade properties. Oxygen forms rare earth oxides. Nitrogen forms nitrides. Hydrogen forms hydrides. Halogens form stable halides. Carbon enters as carbide. Engineers maintain inert conditions during dissolution, stripping, precipitation, calcination, metal reduction, melting, and casting. Even short exposure to air oxidises surfaces. Purification demands gloveboxes, inert gas furnaces, vacuum systems, and continuous gas purification.

The economic barrier remains significant. Ultra high purity circuits require long stage banks, repeated precipitation, controlled redissolution, multiple solvent purification cycles, and high energy input. Throughput remains low. Production cost increases steeply as purity exceeds four nines. Many applications do not require ultra high purity, leading to limited market size for these grades. This reduces incentive for large scale investment in advanced refining technologies.

High purity refinement faces structural barriers arising from chemistry, equipment, impurities, thermodynamics, and economics. These barriers constrain supply, elevate cost, and complicate scale up across the rare earth value chain.

High purity refinement faces kinetic, structural, and process integration barriers that arise once impurity levels fall below one hundred ppm. At these concentrations, impurity behaviour becomes dominated by subtle interactions with ligands, surfaces, interfacial films, and trace degradation products. Refinement ceases to be governed by bulk chemistry and instead depends on micro scale interactions that influence how impurities partition between phases, how complexes form at interfaces, and how trace elements adsorb or desorb from surfaces. Technological barriers emerge when these micro scale effects undermine reproducibility, reduce separation efficiency, or shift equilibrium slightly enough to degrade final purity.

Kinetic barriers arise from slow mass transfer and diffusion limitations in solvent extraction and ion exchange at low concentrations. Rare earth ions exhibit similar diffusivities, and differences in complexation kinetics become small. Achieving high resolution depends on preventing back mixing, stabilising droplet size, and managing interfacial films that impede mass transfer. Impurities such as organic degradation products form interfacial layers that alter droplet coalescence and restrict contact area. These layers mimic surfactants, reducing separation sharpness. Control requires rigorous purification of organic solvents, continuous filtration of both organic and aqueous phases, and elimination of fines that promote unsteady interfaces. Even small amounts of suspended solids cause emulsions that capture trace impurities and reduce stage efficiency.

Surface effects introduce additional barriers. Rare earth complexes adsorb onto equipment surfaces, resin beads, and membrane pores. At low concentrations, adsorption becomes more significant relative to total inventory. Adsorbed impurities re enter solution during process disturbances, stripping, or pH changes. Equipment surfaces accumulate iron, aluminium, and silica residues that act as nucleation sites for precipitation. These deposits contaminate product during downstream steps. Cleaning protocols using acid washes, caustic washes, and chelating agents must remove adsorbed impurities without degrading equipment or leaching contaminants into solution. Resin surfaces also accumulate degradation products that reduce functional group accessibility. Regeneration does not fully restore performance, requiring more frequent replacement.

Chemical stability barriers arise because ligand degradation undermines separation. Organophosphorus extractants degrade through hydrolysis, oxidation, and polymerisation. Degraded ligands bind rare earths differently, shift distribution coefficients, and broaden separation curves. These effects become critical when target purity exceeds four nines. Maintaining extractant stability requires low acidity in organic phase, strict oxygen control, and controlled temperature. Stabilisers improve extractant lifetime but increase cost. Organic phase must be monitored continuously using spectroscopic methods to detect degradation.

Complex equilibria introduce another barrier. Rare earth ions form multiple complexes depending on acidity, ionic strength, and ligand concentration. Complex interconversion depends on small pH shifts that alter speciation. Stripping stages require precise control because slight deviations dissolve adjacent elements. Heavy rare earth complexes remain more stable and require aggressive conditions to strip. These aggressive conditions increase metal hydrolysis and impurity mobilisation. Achieving high purity requires narrow control of pH, temperature, and ligand concentration across hundreds of stages. Automated control systems reduce variability but require continuous calibration.

Mechanical stability of separation equipment introduces further barriers. Mixer settlers require stable hydraulic conditions. Variations in flow rate alter droplet residence time and coalescence behaviour. Phase continuity may shift unexpectedly, altering distribution of impurities. Resin beds expand or contract with temperature and ionic strength, causing channel formation or bed collapse. Membranes warp, swell, or degrade in acidic or chloride rich environments, altering pore structure. Equipment degradation becomes a contamination source. Micro cracks in linings release refractory particles that enter process streams.

High purity precipitation and calcination face additional constraints. Precipitation of rare earth oxalates requires controlled supersaturation to avoid inclusion of impurities within crystal lattices. High purity requires slow nucleation and controlled growth. pH fluctuations cause rapid nucleation that traps impurities. Mixing systems require precise hydrodynamics because dead zones create regions of uncontrolled supersaturation. Calcination requires uniform temperature and oxygen control. Residual carbon, nitrogen, or halides remain in oxide structure if calcination conditions deviate, degrading reduction efficiency.

Metal reduction and casting face further refinement barriers. Rare earth metals absorb hydrogen, nitrogen, and oxygen readily. Even trace contamination prevents formation of required phases in magnets, phosphors, or optical materials. Reduction requires ultra high vacuum or pure inert gas. Furnace contamination introduces unwanted metals. Casting requires controlled solidification to avoid segregation. Minor segregation introduces ppm level impurities that reduce purity below specification. Post reduction purification through vacuum distillation or zone melting improves purity but remains slow and expensive.

Analytical limitations also create barriers. Characterising impurities below ppm requires advanced instrumentation. ICP MS, NAA, and GD MS detect ultra trace elements but require long analysis times and skilled operators. Analytical uncertainty increases as purity increases. Production control becomes slower because feedback cycles depend on analytical data. This delays process adjustment and reduces throughput. High purity refinement requires simultaneous control of micro scale chemistry, surface behaviour, equipment stability, and analytical precision. These barriers become more restrictive as purity targets rise. High purity refinement encounters structural, operational, analytical, and thermodynamic barriers that emerge only at ultra low impurity thresholds. At these levels, impurity transport, ligand behaviour, and equipment interaction follow rules dominated by trace level phenomena rather than bulk chemistry. These barriers define the practical limits of existing refining technologies and shape the cost structure of high end rare earth products used in lasers, magnets, optics, semiconductors, and quantum materials.

Trace impurity behaviour becomes non linear once impurities fall below tens of ppm. Impurities interact with ligands differently at low concentrations, forming transient complexes that differ from bulk species. These transient complexes shift distribution coefficients unpredictably. Iron, aluminium, and silicon form weak complexes at low concentration that escape removal in scrub stages. They accumulate in organic phase through repeated loading cycles, forming stable coordination spheres that mimic rare earth behaviour. Removing these requires ultra selective chelating agents or additional extraction banks. Extractant degradation products at trace levels alter interfacial tension, shifting droplet size distribution and altering coalescence. These effects propagate through mixer settler trains, reducing theoretical plates and widening separation bands.

Equipment micro contamination remains a critical barrier. Stainless steel, polymer linings, and elastomers leach trace metals and organics into process streams. Weld seams release chromium and nickel. Polymer seals release plasticisers. Refractory linings release alumina or silica. These contaminants accumulate in rare earth solutions and alter purity. Mitigation requires exotic materials such as high purity fluoropolymers, glass lined reactors, titanium, or zirconium, increasing cost. Even high purity piping systems accumulate adsorbed rare earths and impurities over time. During process disturbances these desorb into product. Maintaining ultra clean equipment requires frequent acid passivation, replacement of contact surfaces, and controlled rinsing protocols.

Thermodynamic limitations create further barriers. Rare earth species display small differences in Gibbs free energy of complexation across adjacent elements. This limits separation resolution. Heavy rare earth pairs such as Dy–Tb or Tm–Yb require an extreme number of mixer settler stages to achieve separation at ultra high purity. Theoretical plate requirements increase exponentially as target purity approaches five nines. Process disturbances amplify error across long circuits. Even small variations in acidity or temperature accumulate across stages and degrade purity. These limits reflect the fundamental similarity of heavy rare earth ions and constrain process scalability.

Hydrolysis control becomes more difficult at ultra low impurity levels. Rare earth ions hydrolyse at specific pH thresholds. Heavy rare earths hydrolyse at lower pH than light rare earths. Hydrolysed species form colloids that trap impurities. These colloids resist dissolution and migrate through extraction systems, carrying impurities into high purity streams. Colloid control requires filtering through sub micron membranes or stabilising agents that alter hydrolysis behaviour. These stabilisers may introduce additional impurities. Removing stabilisers requires additional steps, increasing complexity.

Crystallisation barriers emerge during oxalate or carbonate precipitation. High purity precipitation demands slow nucleation to avoid entrainment of impurities. Highly pure solutions contain few heterogeneous nucleation sites, increasing supersaturation and causing uncontrolled nucleation. Engineers add seed crystals to control growth, but seed purity must exceed product purity. Producing seed crystals of five nines purity imposes its own barrier. Crystal growth must avoid occlusion of impurities. Mixing must remain uniform to avoid local supersaturation. Precipitates must undergo extensive washing to remove soluble impurities. Washing water purity must exceed product purity to avoid recontamination.

Calcination introduces additional purity constraints. Rare earth oxalates decompose to oxides through intermediate carbonate and oxycarbonate phases. These phases interact with furnace atmospheres. Trace oxygen, moisture, or halogens form surface contaminants. High purity calcination requires ultra clean furnaces, high vacuum, or high purity inert gas. Furnace walls must remain free from contaminants. Heating elements must not release volatiles. Temperature gradients must remain uniform to avoid partial decomposition that traps impurities.

Metal reduction and alloy purification face barriers rooted in reactivity. Rare earth metals absorb hydrogen, nitrogen, and oxygen readily. Even trace contamination reduces conductivity, magnetisation, optical transparency, or phase stability. Metallothermic reduction produces metals containing trace halides. Removing these requires vacuum distillation at high temperatures. Vapour pressure differences between rare earth metals and halides narrow at the heavy end of the series, limiting distillation efficiency. Zone melting improves purity but rare earth metal reactivity complicates zone stability, requiring inert atmosphere and precise thermal control. Surface oxides destabilise molten zones, preventing continuous operation.

Analytical barriers limit refinement. Quality control depends on detecting impurities at sub ppm or even ppb levels. ICP MS suffers from matrix effects. GD MS requires specialised calibration. NAA requires long irradiation times. Analytical uncertainty increases as concentration decreases. Operators cannot adjust process conditions rapidly because feedback cycles depend on slow analytical turnaround. This restricts real time optimisation and increases the cost of quality control.

High purity refinement requires controlling chemical equilibria, surface interactions, equipment contamination, and process stability at unprecedented precision. These barriers reflect fundamental constraints of rare earth chemistry and define the limits of existing industrial technologies.

Printed in Dunstable, United Kingdom